Basic Tools For Beginning Leather Workers

Brian O. Moore

Introduction

Welcome to the world of leatherworking, where skillful hands transform raw hides into works of art and utility. In this book, we embark on a journey into the heart of this timeless craft, uncovering the essential tools and techniques that bring leather to life.

Leatherworking is more than just a craft; it's an art form that spans centuries. Whether you're a novice seeking to explore the beauty of leather or a seasoned artisan looking to refine your skills, this guide is your trusted companion.

Our journey begins with an introduction to the rich array of tools at your disposal. From precision instruments to those that require an artist's touch, each tool plays a vital role in shaping and adorning leather.

As you delve into the intricacies of leatherworking, you'll discover the versatile world of tools designed to perfect the art of finishing, smoothing, and embellishing leather. Explore the palette of colors and finishes that breathe life into your creations, and understand the importance of adhesives and fasteners in securing your designs.

From crafting gouges to precise pricking irons, each tool offers a unique contribution to the art of leatherworking. Gain a comprehensive understanding of their purpose and technique, allowing you to craft with precision and finesse.

Leatherworking is not just a craft; it's an expression of creativity and dedication. Learn the art of tooling, etching, and engraving, as well as the maintenance required to keep your tools in prime condition. Discover the significance of working surfaces that provide the foundation for your leather creations.

In the final chapters, you'll find insights into the world of leatherworking that extend beyond tools. Gain an appreciation for the craftsmanship, attention to detail, and dedication that define this timeless art form.

Join us on this captivating journey into the world of leather tools, where you'll not only master the tools of the trade but also unlock the potential to create leather masterpieces that stand as a testament to your skill and artistry. Let's embark on a path that leads to the mastery of leatherworking—one tool at a time.

Contents

1 - Preface

There are a large number of leather working tools available. Some are very specialized, and others are general. Some are only used for unique styles of leather working, while others will be helpful for any of it.

The great reality of leather working, though, is that it can be started with relatively few tools. This is excellent as you can get a feel for the craft without building out an entire workshop. It also means one can get started without spending a lot of money or investing significant resources early on.

Once you know you'll enjoy it (and you likely will), there are leather working tools available that make every aspect of the craft easier. As your skills and experience grow, so can your set of tools.

One recommendation, as holds true in many things, is buy quality if you can. The performance of better tools is far superior to the very inexpensive ones. You'll find the craftsmanship of your finished work to be so much better, and wonder why some earlier projects were a little rough; was it me or the tools? Likely, the tools.

This also doesn't mean go out and buy the best! A beginning leather worker with the best tools still needs to go through the fun journey of learning and improving their skills (one of the great parts of the craft). Figure out what tools you'll use the most, get some good ones, add over time, and enjoy the journey. Only a handful are really needed to start (knife, awl, needle, thread, hole punch, riveter, & rivets). Many (almost too many), can be added later. Let's take a look.

2 - Awls

Awls are tool with a sharp metal point used for marking or piercing leather. They can be used to impress a small mark such as where belt holes will go, or even dragged across leather to leave a mark such as when tracing pattern templates.

Some come fixed with a single point, others allow points to be interchanged. Points include rounded and diamond shaped, where the diamond shape cuts the leather in such a way that it is easier to stitch through, and also leaves a hole in the leather that can sit more flat once punched.

Awls are a relatively versatile tool for the leatherworker, it's common to have more than one over time.

Awl Haft

A leather awl haft is essentially a handle that can fit interchangeable awl blades. This allows you to have a single handle and multiple blades, instead of many separate awls taking up space on your workspace.

For an awl haft, it's important that the handle is sturdy, and fits comfortably in your hand. The size should feel good. the top of the haft (where it might be struck with a hammer or maul), should have some sort of abrasion protection such as a metal or leather end. This will keep the wooden part of the handle from being damaged when used for a task that requires hitting it with a maul.

Hafts are a handy way to widen your leather working tool set in an efficient way.

Collar Awl

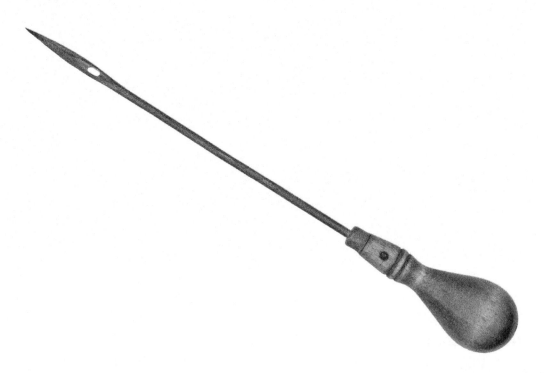

These are usually used by saddle makers. Collar awls feature a long tang (about 8″-10″) with sharp cutting edges on the end. They pierce leather, creating a slit that will allow you to either push or pull thicker lacing through. Since these are generally used for larger holes through ticker leather, the longer design of them helps provide the leverage needed to make the work easier.

Curved Awl

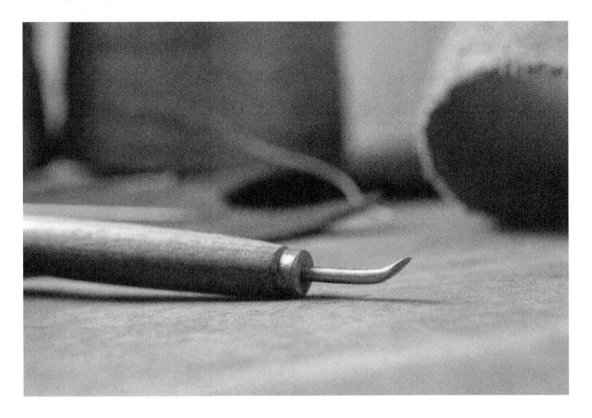

Curved awls are very helpful for creating holes for stitching rounded or curved leather pieces together (as opposed to those that are flat). When joining two pieces that will be over a curved surface, the curved awls create an opening that will more naturally reflect the curve of the final stitch, allowing for tighter stitching and more overall control.

These awls also work well when you don't want to fully penetrate the leather. You can use adjust the pressure applied by hand and go only as deeply into the leather as needed. The curve allows for more agile precision with this task.

Diamond Tip Awl

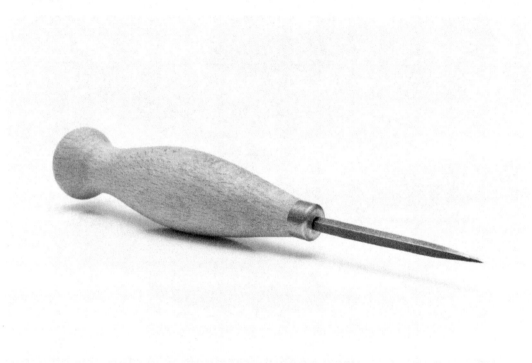

When looking for a tool that can make a hole in leather without leaving a large opening, try a diamond tip awl. They are awls with a diamond-shaped (think 4 corners coming to a point) blade and a very sharp point.

The sharp point allows it to cut into the leather, while the diamond tip pushed through. The result is a tiny "x" cut in the leather. Due to the material flexibility of the "x" cut, when thread passes through along with the additional space needed for the needle, it forms a tight seam. This is better than just a hole punched into the leather, as holes created like that would often be larger than the thread used and leave a loose-fitting seam once complete.

Diamond tip awls come in various sizes so the crafter can choose what size hole is most appropriate for the project. This is definitely a recommended leather working tool.

Lacing Awl

This type of awl is used for pulling leather lacing through holes. The tip usually has a small hooked end, or an eye (like on a needle).

The lacing awl is pushed through the material, lacing hooked onto/through the end, and it's pulled back through the material (with the lacing with it). This is repeated for each hole the lacing will be pulled through.

Needle Awl

A needle awl is an awl with a pointed needle end and an eye on it. This allows threads to be passed through the needle and pushed through leather material when stitching two or more pieces together.

Saddler's Harness Awl

    These awls usually come in an elongated diamond shape. Primarily used by saddle makers, they help make holes in thicker leathers for stitching and sewing. Often available in different sizes, they can be either single awls, or awl bladed that can be fit into a universal awl haft.

Scratch Awls

Scratch awls are pretty universal leather working tools. They have a sharp, rounded point and are used for piercing holes in leather. Coming in a range of sizes, they can be used on thinner leathers or thicker leathers. the holes made can be used for stitching, or most other uses for pierced holes.

These awls can also be used for scratching, or marking, leather. Sometimes when cutting leather or planning where holes will go, it's helpful to leave a mark. Where a pen or pencil might not be the best choice, the scratch awl can be used to leave point marks (for example where a hole might go), or lines (where a cut line might be). Just apply less pressure to the awl by hand and push or drag it across the leather.

Scratch awls and universally helpful leather craft tools.

Sewing Awls

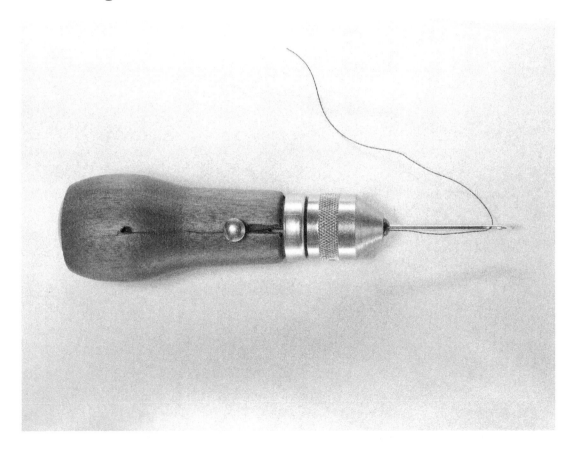

Sewing awls have thread stored within them, making it sewing with them an easy and efficient process.

3 - Burnisher & Slicker Tools

Leather burnishers and slickers are usually rounded or curved tools used to burnish (smooth-out) leather surfaces and edges through friction. Since leather is a natural fiber that has been processed to have a smooth and even finish, when it's cut, the edges will show the internal fibers and often be loose or "hairy" as the fibers stick out.

To help ensure a finished leather product that can wear well and be durable, it is generally good practice to smooth out, or burnish, the edges. This makes them hardened and strong. Sometimes, edges are even painted to seal them up. Many preferences and options are available for this, though burnishers and slickers are often used most.

They come in different materials ranging from plastics to exotic woods. There are hand burnishers, where you move it back and forth over the leather by hand it generates heat through friction and changes the leather surface.

There are also burnishing tools that use motors to rapidly move the burnisher over the leather to seal the edge. Burnishing machines and attachments make this a very easy task, and include dedicated machine as well as attachments that fit onto drills and rotary tools.

The key to burnishing is heat generation and transfer. When the edge leather fibers are heated they join together and smooth out. So friction created by moving a burnisher back and forth quickly makes this happen. When choosing a burnisher material, keep in mind the different heat properties of the material.

Plastic Burnisher

These burnishers are generally the least expensive. They can get hot quickly, which one should keep an eye on, as burnishing too hot or too quickly can burn the leather edge and leave unwanted marks.

Wood Burnisher

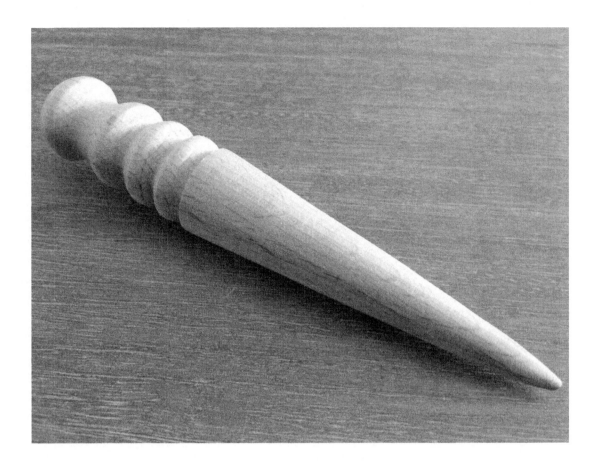

Wood leather burnishers are most popular, as the natural wood material on the natural leather material ends up being a nice combination. The wood doesn't heat too quickly, and the composition of the natural wood finish does a good job of leaving a smooth result on the slicked leather edges.

Brass Burnisher

Brass and other metal burnishers are very strong, though retain a lot of heat. One must be careful when using metal so as to not heat the leather edge too quickly and burn it, leaving unwanted marks. Metal burnishers can also be a little heavier than wood or plastic, though if used on a burnishing machine or rotary tool, this shouldn't be much of an issue.

Glass Burnisher

Glass burnishers and slickers are available as well. Their smooth surface makes it helpful to put a smoothed edge onto leather. Also, glass doesn't retain heat as quickly as other materials, which helps avoid burns on the leather edges.

Exotic Wood Burnisher

Some woods are preferred for their burnishing results. Cocobolo is a very common wood used for this that is strong and durable. It also looks great with a dark natural color to it. Other woods used include paduk, vitae, ebony, pine, oak, maple, rosewood, and most any wood available.

Box Slicker

Instead of a rounded piece of wood or rectangular piece of glass, box slickers a rectangular, solid blocks of wood. The function the same way as other slickers and burnishers through friction created by moving the block quickly over the leather. The shape and size of box slickers can be of preference to some crafters, based on what they're working on and how they like to work.

Power Burnisher Machine

If you love burnishing, or need to often if you're making higher-volume production leather work, a power burnisher machine might be for you. It is essentially a motor with various burnishing mounts. Since it is powered by electricity, the about of manual effort on the crafter is very much reduced, mainly to holding the leather piece gently by the burnisher.

Dedicated tabletop burnishing machines might have attachments on each side of a motor to hold wood burnishers, sand paper, plastic burnishing tip, or an array of burnishing finishers. Rotary tools, such as Dremels, can also work very well as powered burnishers. They're handles which makes maneuvering it around the leather quite easy.

As another option, burnisher attachments for power drills are widely available. This can quickly make any home drill (corded or cordless) into a burnisher very easily. Just remember, all that power can easily burn the leather edge! Burnish slowly, and safely

Water Spray Bottle

Sometimes it helps burnishing when the leather or leather edge is wet first. Not too wet and soaked, but just enough to aid in the heating and smoothing process the burnishers do. A common water spray bottle can be great here as a leather working tool, allowing the crafter to mist the leather areas just a little and then get to burnishing.

They don't spill easily, and some have an adjustable spray nozzle so you can choose how much water comes on in the mist. A simple but convenient way to wet leather to be burnished.

4 - Cleaning & Conditioning

Leather is a natural material and can last for centuries if it is well-cared for. That usually involves periodic cleaning and conditioning to ensure that it stays in top shape during everyday use.

Leather needs to maintain a healthy balance of humidity and oils. If it gets too dry it can become brittle and flake and crack apart. If it gets too wet it can begin to mold and decompose. It very much likes the middle ground of just enough moisture and oil to be a supple, strong material that lasts.

Leather Cleaner

Choosing a leather cleaner is highly dependent on the type of leather being cleaned. There are specialized leather cleaners and more general ones that are safe for many leathers. The cleaner helps to loosen and remove dust, dirt, debris, and grime from the leather surface. This ensures that when you apply the conditioner, it's not trapping any dirt in, and instead going right into the leather where it needs to be.

Be sure to check that whatever cleaner you might use is safe for the type of leather being used on. And always try it on a small, out of sight place first on the leather to test for any potential adverse reactions or issues with the cleaner and the specific piece of leather you're using it on.

Leather Conditioner

After cleaning, the application of leather conditioner helps to rehydrate the leather and put back in moisture and oils that are essential to its maintenance.

Some conditioners also leave a protective finish over the leather, further helping it to be resistant to picking up too much water, dirt, and debris before the next time it is cleaned and conditioned. When well-cared for, leather can last and be usable for generations.

Leather Oil

Leather oil is a type of leather conditioner. There are many different types and formulations available. Some cater to specific leather products (shoes, boots, bags, etc.). Others to the conditions the leather will be used in. And even others that have more general formulations that work well on most leathers.

Leather oils can be just oils, or combinations of oils, waxes, and other natural and/or synthetic ingredients aimed at conditioning and protecting the leather. Definitely read up on the particular oil you might choose, reviews of it's performance, and how well it will work for your specific leather application. With the right oil/conditioning, the leather will look and feel amazing.

5 - Creaser/Folder Tools

Leather creasers help put a crease in the edge of leather, often for aesthetic reasons. They can also be used for functional reasons when folding/shaping leather goods, or putting an edge onto fine leatherwork.

For projects where thick leathers are being used and there is a fold line, the creaser/folder can be used to prepare the line on which the fold will bend. This avoid stretching the leather near the bend, making it much cleaner and visually appealing.

Creaser/Folder

Manual creasers can be drawn by hand against the leather. An example is putting the visual touch of a thin line near the outside edge of a belt. In some cases the creaser can be heated so it runs more smoothly over and deeper into the leather, and more easily crease softer leathers.

Creasers can also be used, instead of burnishing, to put an edge onto leatherwork. An example is finishing the edges of a wallet, or those on a luxury handbag.

Creaser/Embosser Machine

When working on a project that benefits from a heated creaser, there is a machine to the rescue! The electric creaser machine feeds electricity to a hand-held creaser. On the end is metal tip that gets warm from the electricity, and delivers a consistent temperature over the leather.

When finishing the edges naturally or with added protectants such as wax, al electric creaser will make a huge difference. These are often used on very high-end leather work.

Edge Creaser

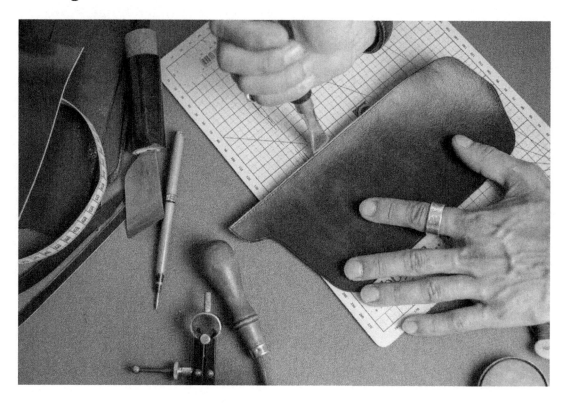

The Edge creaser allows for consistent application of edge lines at fixed widths on leather items. They can be heated first, to make the edge lines easier to press, or used without heat for making lighter indentation lines.

6 - Knives and Bladed Tools

So very common in leather craft is cutting leather. In most things you'll work on, cutting will be some part of the process or design. As such, getting familiar with the different types of cutting and bladed leather tools will be helpful.

They include knives in many varieties, shapes, and sizes. Rotary cutters are rounded blades mounted as a wheel, scissors for rougher cutting, and strap cutters for cutting long leather straps and laces. Within each type are various configurations, sizes, and qualities to fit your needs.

With all knives and bladed tools, proper maintenance is important. Leather can be a tough material, knives with sharp, well-cared-for blades will make the work much easier. and the end result will be much cleaner and professional looking. Now on the to the fun stuff and all the info!

Knives

The staple leather working tool is the knife. There are so many variations that are used in so many ways. In some cases the only tool one might need for leather craft project is just a knife.

So where to begin? Like most things, simply. The most basic knives (such as utility and crafting knives) can go a long way. As your skills in leather craft evolve, you'll get a better feel for what specialized knives might work best for the type of leather working you do. You'll also develop a preference for what types/style you like best.

Xacto Knife

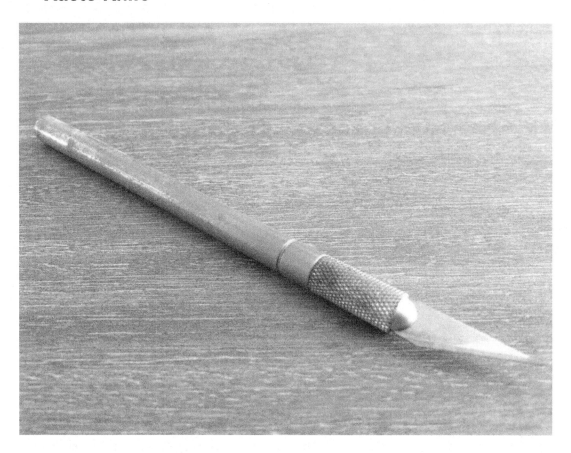

This is a handheld knife with replaceable metal blades. The blades come in different shapes, sizes, and angles for almost any crafting and cutting need. New blades are very sharp, reliable, and not too expensive. To replace a blade, just unscrew the base of the knife, remove the old blade, put a new one in, and re-tighten the base. Xacto knives/blades are very handy for leather working.

Utility (Box Cutter) Knife

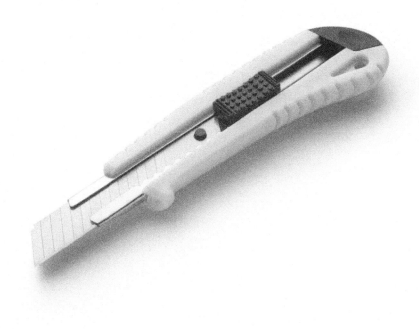

Box cutters can work great for leather working too. Some come with replaceable blades. Others come with multiple blades where once one is dull, just snap it off and the new, sharp blade is available. Often inexpensive, this is definitely a viable option when getting into leather craft.

Round Knife/Head Knife

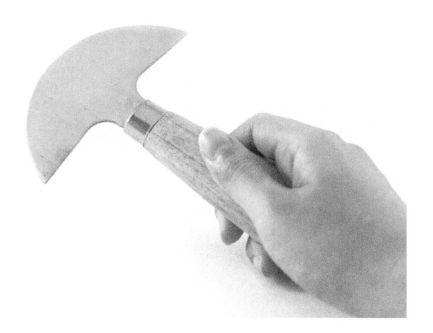

The round knife, also referred to as a head knife, is one of the most versatile knifes for leather working. It consists of a large, 1/2 circle blade that is sharp on the rounded portion. Since it has such a large blade surface and cutting edge, it can more effectively cut through thicker leathers than smaller knives.

Head knives also work well for thin leathers and detailed cutting. The maneuverability of the blade edge make it useful for cutting curves. The blade depth can also be controlled manually to set lines into the leather without cutting fully through.

Round knives come in many brands and qualities. Handle shapes are important too. You want to have one that feels comfortable in the hand, in all the various positions one might hold it while cutting. Given all of the assets of the larger, sharper blade, one must also be very careful when handling and using a head knife. with proper safety and use, it is excellent. This is another of the top leather craft tools to have.

Swivel Knife

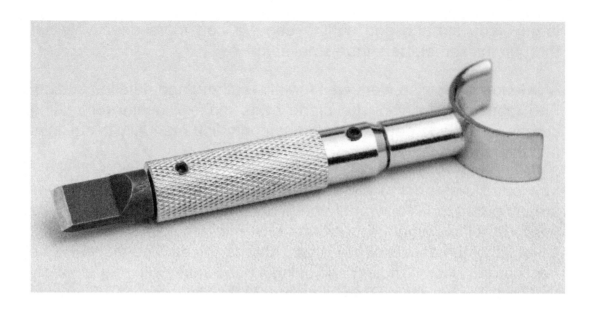

The swivel knife is used for leather tossing and carving intricate patterns into leather pieces. Usually made of metal, sometimes brass, they have a chisel-edged blade and are held upright in the hand. On the top is a curved piece of metal that acts as a finger rest, so the index finger can lay across the top and help control the angle and pressure applied to the blade.

Blades styles can vary from straight to angled, each benefitting different cutting style and uses. It takes some time to learn and master the swivel knife. Once familiar with the techniques, one can craft some incredibly detailed and impressive decorative work into leather.

Flat Knife

The flat knife is a style of knife with a long, thin, metal blade that extends through a long, flat handle. The cutting edge is very similar to the xacto knife blades, with angled and flat edge options available.

The edge can be re-sharpened for a long time, making it a good investment. The metal handle also adds a comfortable weight to the knife's movement in the hand. The flatness of the handle helps gives it good control.

On of the most popular flat knives is the "L'Indispensable" made by Vergez Blanchard. It even offers unique angling to the blades better suited for right, or left handed users. Pretty amazing the precision is that accurate that left or right handed options are even available for a blade. Worth checking out if you want to invest in a high-quality knife.

Bevel Point

Beveled point leather working knives have a beveled edge to the blade. This helps for skiving and edge trimming where you want a little more control over how deep the cut is and how the path of the blade moves through the cut.

For example, you might want to cut fairly deep into the edge and taper it up as you move forward. You might want to taper a cut out as you move along an edge, or even just shave a tine bit of leather from a surface when doing finishing work. The beveled shape of the blade will help with this.

Curved Lip

Curved lip knives, usually made of steel, are often used by cobblers doing shoe repair. Often designed to be right or left handed for use, they have a uniquely shaped bent tip with a sharp edge that allows for easy trimming of show soles.

It is important to find one with a comfortable handle that fits well within the hand. This is not as common as other leather cutting tools, and usually intended for specialized uses.

Trimming Knife

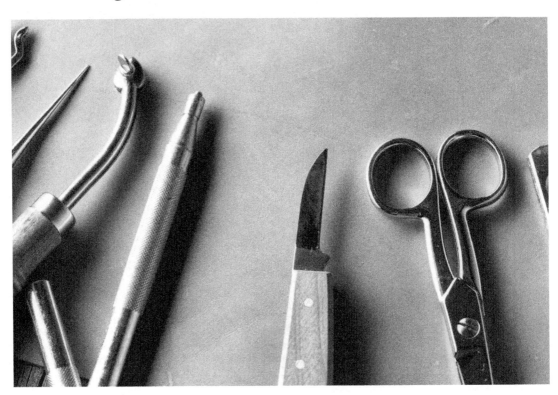

Trimming knives are used for finer, detailed leather work. They are available with both straight and curved blades. When cutting out intricate patterns, trimming thread, or working on smaller details including edge, seam, and trim work, this is a great choice to have in the leather craft tool kit.

Sharp Point Knife

The sharp point knife features a long (maybe 6"-8") steel blade with a curved end. This gives the blade more cutting surface and control over curved cuts, making it a great choice for cobblers and shoemakers. This style knife also works very well when cutting through thicker leathers, as the larger blade surface makes that sometimes difficult task much easier.

Curved Blade Trim Knife

This is a specialized type of trimming knife that allows for more agility in cuts. It can make curved cutting easier, as well as more nimble movements through other detailed work such as edge finishing. This trim knife can also be used for trimming threads and working on intricate patterns.

Straight Knife

Leather working straight knives have a long, straight blade. It might taper on an angle in from the tip, though the sharpened blade portion is straight. These knives work great for cutting very accurately in leather craft, and the blade can sit securely and deeply into the leather throughout the cutting process.

A comfortable handle is important on a knife like this, as the broader cutting style used benefits from resting well in the hand.

Shoemaker's Knife

Shoemakers knives are a specialized leather working knife. They are often made of solid metal and work for a variety of needs including overall cutting, skiving, scraping, large trimming, and shaping the soles of shoes.

These come in versions that are straight, or curved. The curved versions come in left-handed and right-handed styles. The straight versions are usually double-beveled to be used in either hand. Overall lengths are usually 10"-12" long.

Rand Knife/Welt Knife

The rand knife/welt knife is another cobbler/shoemaker's specialty knife. Available in right or left-handed versions, it has a uniquely angled blade that makes it useful for trimming the leather soles of shoes. They are particularly helpful for trimming around the heel area. This is the kind of knife that might not get used often, though will help produce excellent results when it does.

Channel Knife

Another cobbler/shoemaker's specialty knife, the Channel knife is used primarily for cutting a channel into the insole of the shoe leather. The blade has a curve to it that helps it rest just right into and through the leather while cutting.

Paring Knife

Leather paring knifes really shine in the bookbinding craft. They come in a variety of sizes and blade types including rounded, angled, and straight.

French pairing knives generally have a semi-rounded blade with an upright handle. Swiss pairing knives feature a similarly rounded blade, though don't have the handle, just the extension of the metal from the blade to hold on to.

English pairing knives look like very large leather cutting flat knives, where the end has an angled blade and the metal from the blade continues up and is essentially the handle. These knives are available both right-handed and left-handed versions.

German pairing knives are a mix of the other styles. They feature a long blade with a curved end, offering the versatility and agility of a curved blade along with a straight portion that extends up until it reaches the handle, made of a well-finished wood.

Rotary Cutters

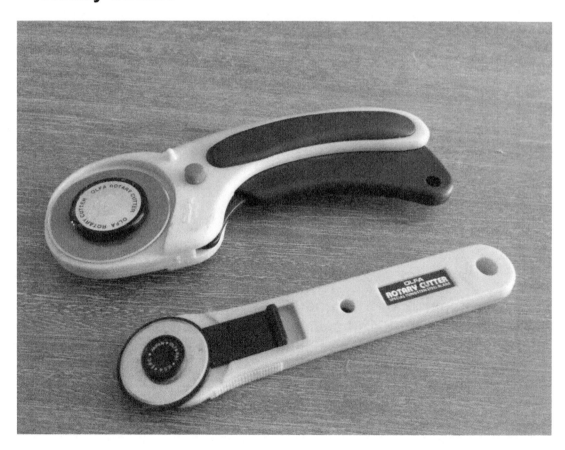

Rotary cutters are tools with circular blades that can be continuously pushed or pulled to make cuts into fabrics, leathers, and many materials. Since the blades rotate, they can cut along curves very easily, making them a great option for more complex designs.

Rotary cutters also cut straight lines very well, usually when used with a straight edge as a guide. Blades are as share as other knife style blades, and can be sharpened often and replaces when necessary. This is a great tool when looking for something beyond a fixed blade knife.

Cut-Resistant Gloves

Cut-resistant gloves help protect the wearers hand from cuts when working with or around sharp knives. The level of cut resistance can vary based on the materials, methods of manufacture, and intended level of protection.

They would be a recommended addition to your leather working tool kit, where both or one can be work, whenever appropriate. For example, if the right hand is holding a cutting knife and the left holding the leather, maybe wear a cut resistant glove on the left hand as that will be nearer the cutting blade.

Leather crafters have gone for centuries without them, and they're not an absolute need. Though it's always helpful to be protected if reasonable and in some cases these can help.

Strap Cutters

Leather strap cutters are a hand-held, wooden device with a mounted leather blade that cut long leather straps from larger pieces of leather and hide. For example, if you want to make a belt from a large leather hide, a strap cutter can be used to cut off a long length of leather in a consistent thickness. It can also be used for making leather laces. Some versions are referred to as "ploughs"

There is a means to adjust the thickness of the preferred cut, usually marked with measurements for easy reference. Blades must be kept sharp, and are replaceable if needed. Once the thickness is set, the leather is lined up and manually pulled through.

As that happens, it is cut in the thickness set, and the result is the original big piece of leather, and a strap in just the width you want it. There is a classic design of this that has been around for years that is very common and useful.

Strap Cutter Machine

When doing higher-volume or repetitive strap cutting, a machine is available to definitely help. These come in both manually operated versions (hand crank) and electrically-powered versions.

The width of the cut is set, the leather positioned, then mechanically drawn through the cutter resulting in straps or laces just the way you need them. These are definitely more expensive than the hand-held strap cutters, though likely worth it if you plan on doing a lot of work that involves straps or laces.

Leather Scissors

Scissors usually have symmetrically-sized finger holes and are shorter than 6" in length. They can be held in the air while cutting, or rested on the cutting surface while making the cut. Leather cutting scissors are usually made with strong, sharp blades that can smoothly handle thinner and thicker leathers when cutting.

Leather Shears

Shears are usually longer than 6" in length and have asymmetrically-sized finger holes, one is larger than the other to more comfortably fit four fingers. The thumb can comfortably rest in the smaller hole. Sometimes shears are intended to rest on and flow along the cutting surface for smooth, stable cuts.

Leather cutting scissors are usually made with strong, sharp blades that can smoothly handle the thinner and thicker leathers that require a bit of heft when making cuts.

Thread Scissors

Thread scissors will most likely be helpful if you're hand-sewing or machine-sewing a fair amount of your leather work. They are usually small, only a few inches long, with small, very sharp blades.

Their size allow them to get into tough-to-reach places and angles, who their sharpness will shear the thread leaving a crisp end without frays. Thread scissors can also help during edging and finishing if you need to trim any extra long fibers that come up on the leather's edge after a cut.

Lacing Cutter

Lacing cutters are specialized versions of strap cutters, in that they are intended only for lace cutting (smaller widths of leather). They usually allow for cuts up to about 3", and down to about 1/8". This is good for most straps and strips that will be used for laces, belts, braiding lace, fringe, and tie-straps.

Lacing cutters come in both hand-held, and table-top versions. The table-top versions usually secure to the table, making it easier to pull the lacing through. This is especially helpful with more frequent or high volume work.

Leather Working Clicker Press

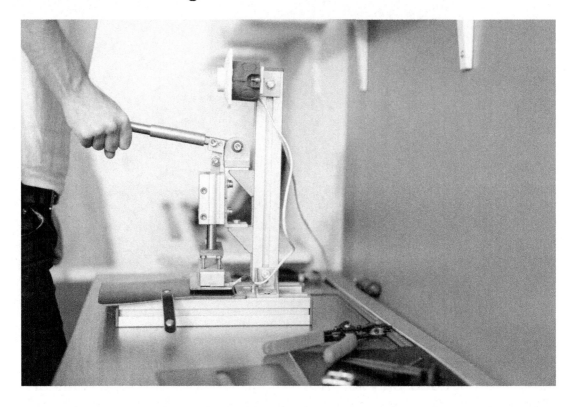

A clicker press is a tool that applies tremendous force to a small area in order to cut out designs in leather. They fit on a tabletop, have a base, usually several cutting board surfaces, and a lever that drives the press.

Due to leverage, when the lever is pressed by hand, it generates literally tons of force onto a very small ares through a die. The dies are metal, and pre-formed into a shape. For example a rosette, a shape, or even wallet pieces.

The benefit of a clicker press, with its related dies, is that a specific cut in leather can be done much faster than by hand. They can also effectively cut through thicker leathers with ease. Clicker presses are relatively expensive, though for the leather worker that is producing similar products in volume, it can certainly help with scale, productivity, and efficiency.

Leather Cutting Dies

Leather cutting dies are pre-formed, metal shapes with a sharp cutting edge, used to cut shapes out of leather. They are laid on top of leather material, and struck with a maul, mallet, or hammer. The force drives the sharp edges into the leather, resulting in a cut out piece in the shape of the die.

Dies are helpful when one finds themselves cutting many of a similar pattern out by hand. An example is a wallet maker with a great design. They need many pieces to produce a lot of wallets, though cutting them out one by one by hand can be time consuming.

Leather cutting dies can be custom made to any shape or size. Generally they can be put into a clicker press for even easier cutting, or manually stuck by hand. Although there's usually an initial investment to make or purchase a die, if it will get used often it is usually a worthwhile investment.

7 - Dyes, Paints, & Finishes

Leather paints, dyes, and finishes help turn leather into some many incredible products. From the uncolored hyde, or un-dyed finished leathers, the possibilities are endless when considering what your final piece can look like.

Leather dyes are pigments used to change the overall color of leather. Paints are generally used as accent colors on locations such as edges. Finishes can be both visually appealing, to transparent and protective, helping the leather to wear well and last longer.

Wool Daubers

Wool daubers are little balls of wool attached to a wire handle. The balls are approximately 1/2" – 1" wide, and the wire handle about 5" long. Daubers are great for dipping into leather dyes and finishes, then rubbing onto the leather surface to apply the dye or finish.

The wool picks up an amount of dye or finish depending on how deeply it is dipped. It then offers an amount of control over where the dye or finish is placed on the leather piece and how evenly it is applied. For smaller leather pieces, dauber are a great choice as an applicator.

Leather Edge Paint

Leather edges need to be finished after cutting, in order to strengthen the edge and protect the leather inside. Usually, burnishing is done to seal the edge. For additional protection, and mainly visual appeal, edge paint can be applied.

Edge paint covers the edges of leather goods and items, sealing the inside of the edge, and providing a pleasant finish to look at once it dries. Some leather crafters use this to create contrast with the leather piece. Others use it to blend the edges in. Edge paint are available in a wide variety of colors.

Leather Deglazer

Leather deglazer is a chemical combination that is used to prepare leather for dyeing. Processed leathers, or even finished leather goods, often come with protective finishes on them. Deglazer, once applied to the leather, helps strip away the existing finish and any additional residues or chemicals underneath it.

With previous finishes removed, the leather is ready to be dyed a different color, or have a different finish applied. Deglazers are usually highly toxic and require outdoor ventilation for safe use. They are also temperature sensitive, and should be used within the temperature range recommended on any specific deglazer you're using.

Leather Dye

Leather dyes are pigments mixed with a base (usually alcohol, oil, or water), and applied to leather to change it's color. Each types has it's own performance characteristics, so use would depend on personal preference and the specific project on which they're being used.

For best results when dyeing leather, a crafter can usually always dye darker, though not lighter. For example, one can dye a vegetable tanned belt gray. Then brown. Then black. However, they can't nearly as easily dye a black leather belt a lighter color such as gray, or white.

In general, dyeing leather requires proper ventilation to ensure a safe working environment. Also, leather dyes are temperature sensitive, and should be used within the temperature range recommended on any specific dye that you're using.

Leather Dye – Alcohol-Based

Alcohol-based leather dyes penetrate the leather deeply, so the color goes beyond the surface. The colors are usually vibrant. However, after the dye is applied and the alcohol dries, it takes some of the moisture out of the leather along with it.

Leathers dyed with alcohol-based types when then usually benefit from application of a leather conditioner to restore some of that pliability and the oils within the piece. Often, dyed leathers are coated with a finishing coat, to seal in the dye, prevent it from rubbing off, and protect the leather overall.

Leather Dye – Oil-Based

Oil-based leather dyes penetrate the leather deeply, so the color goes beyond the surface. The colors are usually vibrant. Since these dyes are oil-based, less moisture is pulled from the leather when drying than with alcohol-based dyes.

Alcohol-based dyed leather when then usually benefit from application of a conditioner to restore some of that pliability before a finish is added. Often, dyed leathers are coated with a finishing coat, to seal in the dye, prevent it from rubbing off, and protect the leather overall.

Leather Dye – Water-Based

Water-based leather dyes don't penetrate the leather as deeply than other dye types, and the colors aren't usually as vibrant. However, they are generally less toxic than the other types.

As with most dyed leather, even though these dyes include moisture, it can be helpful to coat with a leather finish after dyeing. This will help protect the color from rubbing off, and protect the leather from excessive wear.

Leather Wax

Leather wax is a wax, or oily compound that is used as a leather finisher. It often is blended with oils and conditioners. When applied to the leather, it helps add moisture and also protect the surface from daily use.

Usually after applying, the leather wax is buffed out to a shine (matte or gloss depending on the formulation). It leave a smooth, protective surface over the leather that is resistant to dirt, grim, and water.

Leather Edge Paint Roller

An edge paint roller is a uniquely designed paint applicator for adding paint to leather edges. Some products have very fine edges, such as wallets and watch bands. Other project have larger edges such as briefcases and bags.

Using a small paint brush to apply paint is do-able, though requires detailed concentration and an even application across a usually long surface. In comes the edge paint roller. It is a round, tapered metal tip that can spin/roll. The tip is dipped into the paint, and then rolled across the leather edge. This leaves an even, consistent layer of paint. Perfect!

Edge paint rollers can be cleaned, reused, and are definitely a helpful leather working tool for someone that prefers and performs a fair amount of edge painting.

8 - Edger & Beveler Tools

Edgers and bevelers are tools used to shave the square edges off of leather. This is both for functional an aesthetic purposes. Functionally, it removes the sharper square edges and leaves a more rounded edge to the leather. This makes it less likely to catch on other items during daily use. The rounded edges are also more comfortable on items that are handled frequently such as belts and wallets.

Aesthetically, the rounded edges on leather are generally more pleasing to the eye. They soften the look and also make it easier to seal the edges when they are burnished or edge-painted.

Edgers and burnishers come in many different shapes, sizes, and styles. They are usually made with metal blades/tips attached to a wooden handle.One thing to keep in mind is that not all edgers are sized in the same way. A particular size from one brand or manufacturer might not match that from another manufacturer.

Similar to clothes, it's best to try out the ones you'd like, and ensure the sizing meets your needs. In general, it is important to keep the edges sharp to ensure smooth, clean cuts.

Leather Bisonnette Edge Beveler

The bisonnette edge beveler is a beveling tool that has a rounded cutting hole towards the tip. While most edgers have a uni-directional cutting edge that needs to be pushed away from the body to make a cut, this one can be either pushed or pulled due to the circular cutting hole.

This makes it a convenient option for edging. They come in various sizes, so preference on edger operation, and cutting size will help determine if this works well for you.

Leather Common Edge Beveler

The common edge beveler is, well, the most common beveler type. It features a v-shaped blade with a rounded center, perfect for taking the edges off of leather pieces. These are a standard leather working tool, and work great across so many projects.

Available sizes vary greatly, as well as qualities and handle materials. Also, the feel between manufacturers can vary too, so it's important to try different ones out while determining which feels best to you.

Leather Push Beader

The push header is a more specialized tool used mainly in leather carving and decorative leather working. Their primary function is to imprint in the leather two parallel lines with a rounded "bead" that runs down the middle of them.

They can usually be either pushed or pulled. If you're looking to add some visual appeal to your projects, the push header might be a helpful leather working tool addition.

Leather French Edge Beveler

French edge bevelers feature a more square-shaped scoop edge. They can be used for some edging work, though also work well for gouging or skiving. Generally they are universal and can be used either right-handed or left-handed. these bevelers are good options when looking for straighter edge cuts, or to shave down/remove material.

Leather Wheel Beveler

Wheel bevelers are used to efficiently bevel patterns into the leather. They have a rotating metal wheel on the end of a wooden handle. The wheel is generally imprinted with a pattern or design that then rolls into the leather when pushed or pulled. They can be a handy tool that make beveling decorative patterns much easier.

Leather Round Edger

These edgers are a type of general leather edger, great for both straight and curved cutting. They feature a rounded blade that helps achieve smooth, round edges, without leaving edger lines/marks. The edger marks are sometimes visible when using the common bevelers.

This is a nice tool to have when working on finer projects or softer leathers.

Leather Strap Edger Tabletop Machine

The tabletop strap edger works similar to other edgers, though it gives more consistent results. With manual edgers it's important to be as steady as possible when using them, as variations in the manual pressure can lead to slightly higher or deeper edges along the leather piece.

The tabletop edger has two sets of blades that each edge an opposite of a leather strap. The blades are set, and strap pulled through as they edge. Since it's a fixed machine with fixed blades, the edge will be even on both sides, and along the length of the edged strap or belt. This is really helpful if you're doing a higher volume work and seek consistent edging results in an efficient, slightly more automated way.

9 - Finishing Tools

Leather finishing tools are used primarily to refine the edges of leather work. When cut, the natural fibers inside leather are exposed. They might show as loose or "hairy" as the fibers stick out. This is generally unpleasing to the eye, and also exposes the leather to faster wear and damage from moisture.

Finishing the edges helps to smoothen and seal the fibers. This makes the edges stronger, protects the leather, and is more visually appealing. Leather can be finished using a combination of abrasion/friction and waxes/sealers.

Sandpaper/Sanding Blocks

Sandpaper can be used on newly cut leather to smoothen the edges. The roughness of the sandpaper wears down the loose fibers, shortening them and creating a more dense, smoother surface.

This is usually achieved by using coarser sandpapers that are rougher, and working down to finer sandpapers that leave a tighter edge. Sandpaper is available is many variations, most commonly grit size. Grit size refers to the size of sand grains on the paper. Coarser grits have a lower number (for example, 50), while finer grits have a higher number (for example, 120).

Sanding blocks are blocks of material, usually wood or plastic, with sandpaper attached. It can make it easier to hold and rub across the leather when attached to something that fits well into the hand.

Sandpaper is relatively inexpensive and is quite useful for leather finishing.

Beeswax

Beeswax is a natural wax produced by bees. It has numerous functions in leather working, including leather finishing. It can be used to condition leather, and also applied as a protectant that provides water resistance and in some cases water proofing properties.

Beeswax can also be applied to the edges of leatherwork to form a strong barrier. It protects the underlying leather and provides a smooth finish. Warming the wax during application helps it flow into the leather for effective adhesion, while also allowing it to be shaped during burnishing.

This is a versatile finishing substance that most crafters will find use for depending on the project.

Leather Burnishing Gum

Burnishing gum is a substance with similar to properties to beeswax. It is used to coat the edges of leather work to protect the underlying leather and seal the edge from outside elements and wear. Burnishing gum also leaves a smooth, shiny surface on the leather edge that is quite visually appealing.

They're generally available in synthetic and some more natural varieties. While beeswax is more commonly used, burnishing gums offer alternative options with sometimes different properties.

Piece of Canvas

Canvas material pieces can be used, similar to sandpaper, to abrade the edges of leather. It can help "mat" down the look leather fibers on an edge, giving it a more smooth appearance. While using canvas along likely wouldn't be the only method applied, it can be used in conjunction with other finishing methods to produce nice edges.

Carnauba Wax

Carnauba wax is a formula that can be applied to leather. It is usually a blend of waxes and conditioners. When applied, it serves to condition the leather while also providing a protective layer that helps resist dirt, grime, and moisture.

The wax is usually put on by hand, then buffed to a shine. The end result is a soft-feeling, shiny surface that wears well and looks great.

Leather Resolene

Resolene is a synthetic finish for leather. While waxes can be used to seal and protect leather, resolene is comprised of acrylic. It is usually applied in thin layers, each building a thinner layer of acrylic. When dried, it will result is a smooth, durable, shiny surface that provides a fair amount of protection for the underlying leather. Resolene is available in several colors, so a match can be made closely to the leather color that is being coated.

Hand Leather Rougher

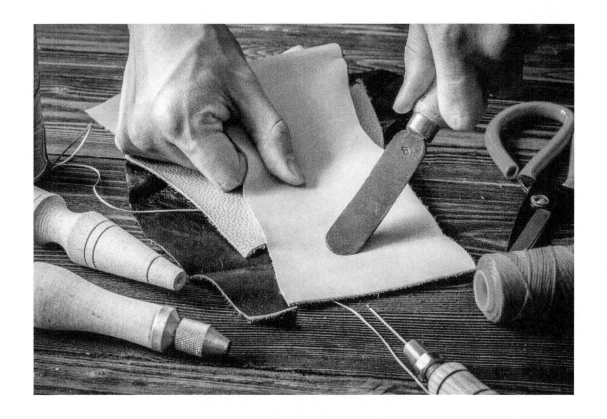

In some application and on some projects, an effective way of joining leather can be via glueing. In order to help ensure a strong bond between surfaces, glues generally benefit from having a rough area on which to form their bond.

When finished leathers are mostly smooth, a hand leather rougher tool digs into and scratches up the leather, creating a rough surface. This newly-roughed surface will greatly help the adhesive set into and join the leather pieces once dried. Hand roughers are relatively common in saddle making and related work.

Alcohol Heating Lamp

Metal leather creasers can be used for both functional and aesthetic purposes. They generally perform better when heated, as they more smoothly mark and glide into the leather, forming the creases.

Alcohol heating lamps are a common way to heat up these creasing tools while working on leather craft projects. They are usually comprised of a small metal reservoir filled with denatured alcohol, that when lit, provides a steady flame. Usually attached is a metal extension where the creasing tool can rest while it is heating on the flame.

If maintained properly and watched closely during use, alcohol-based heating lamps can be an easy way to heat your creasing tools right by your leather working space.

Metal Files

When finishing leather edges (to seal and protect them), many abrasives can be used. Along with sandpaper, metal files are another option. With so many varieties available (round, flat, diamond, etc.). They are also available in many grit sizes. For grit sizes, the smaller the size number, the larger/rougher the filing result will be. Likewise, the larger the number the more fine/smooth the filing result will be.

Generally, one would start with a rougher file and work their way down to a finer file as he edge becomes tighter and smoother. Files make it easy to smooth rough leather edges, helping prepare them for further finishing such as burnishing, waxing, or painting.

10 - Glues & Adhesives

While leathers are typically joined via methods including sewing or riveting, sometimes it can be helpful to first secure the surfaces with a glue or adhesive. Once in position, it makes it easier to do the sewing, riveting, etc.

There are many different types of adhesives available that work well with leather. Some are temporary, with a tacky result that can be easily moved and reapplied. Others are stronger and more difficult to remove. Some glues expand into the materials as they dry. And yet others are extremely strong, considered permanent. For very strong glues, they bind so tightly that trying to remove the adjoined pieces will likely damage the leather.

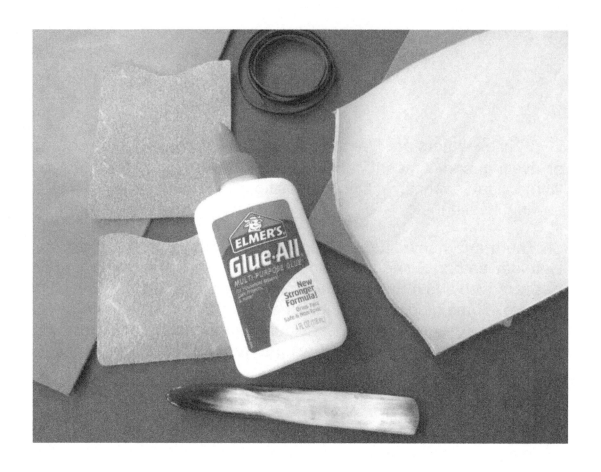

Wool daubers can be used to help apply and smooth out leather glues. It's important to know the preferred end result. If you plan to remove stitching at a later point and separate leather pieces, consider using a less strong, or temporary adhesive to make this easier. Glues are available with different drying times, and some variation in colors.

Glue Spreaders

Leather glue spreaders are commonly a flat-edged tool made of plastic. They allow for even spreading of glues over flat surfaces, allowing the layers to be very thin, or glue focus on a particular spot. after used, they can be washed and reused, as maintaining the clean edge is very important to a smooth spreading of the glue.

Glue brushes are also an options when spreading glue. They are dipped into a liquid adhesive and then applied to the leather. They allow larger volumes of glue to be applied more quickly, though aren't as precise as the glue spreaders. The spreaders are an easy way to target glue placement and preferred volume.

Glue Pot

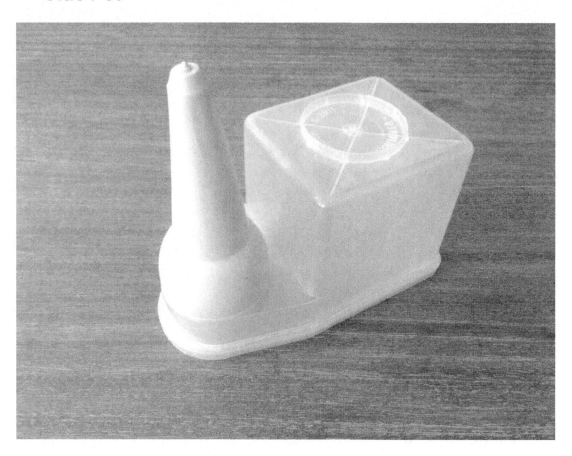

Glue can be a really helpful addition to your leather working tool set, though a common issue is that they dry out quickly if sitting out open while you work. A glue pot is a small plastic holder for adhesives that is air tight. Glues can be stored for long period of time in glue pots.

When you want to use the glue, an air-tight cap unscrews open, revealing a brush and portion of the glue. The brush can be dipped into the exposed glue and applied to the leather. Once finished, just screw the air tight cap back on and the glue will remain in great shape for the next use. Glue pots are a helpful tool to have if you do a fair amount of glueing while working with leather projects.

Leathercraft Cement

Leathercraft cement is a type of adhesive specifically made for leather craft use. It helps make strong bonds in an easy-to-use formula. Positives are that they are generally non-toxic, non-flammable, and dry relatively quickly. This is worth keeping in mind as some adhesives can be toxic to breath in requiring proper ventilation when working. Leathercraft cement can be useful across leather types and project needs.

Leather Working Metal Roller

Leather working metal rollers are used to smooth out layers of leather that are glued together. Since leather can be thick, and also usually has a nicely finished, smooth surface, a special tool is helpful here.

The metal roller is comprised of a solid, heavy metal cylinder attached to a handle. When pushed or pulled, the roller rolls over the leather, applying pressure and helping ensure a tight adhesion between leather layers. Bubbles and air gaps are removed, which contributes to a nicely-finished and fine looking end result.

Wire Brush

The wire brush is a tool that can be used to help roughen the surface of leather prior to gluing. The rougher surface can help with better glue adhesion then if it were to be applied to a smooth surface.

11 - Gouge Tools

Leather gouges are used to remove a bit of the leather material in order to allow the leather to fold or bend in a preferred direction. Since when leather bends the fibers would stretch, removing some of the material at the bend point allows the leather to more naturally fold over, creating a visually appealing, and functionality helpful element to the design. Leather gouges come in a few different shapes.

Adjustable V-Gouge

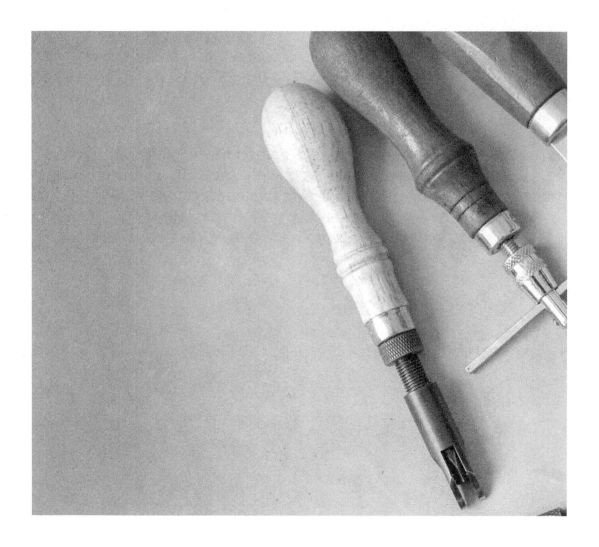

A leather v-gouge is pushed into leather to carve out a consistent line of material somewhat deeply into the leather piece. Depth can usually be adjusted on the gouge tool itself. The v-shape of the blade is preferred for and helpful in making sharp, right-angle folds in handbags, laptop cases, notebooks, travel bags, and other leather goods with right angles in their design.

Adjustable U-Gouge

The u-gouge has a u-shaped blade that works well for cutting grooves into leather. The depth of the groove can usually be adjusted on the tool, allowing for accurate depth control based on the specific project you're working on. the groove it cuts will allow leather to be more easily bent around corners, which helps with a variety of leather goods styles including bag making and case making. If needed, the u-gouge can sometimes be used as a stitch groover, adding to it's versatility.

12 - Groover Tools

Leather groovers are tools used to cut grooves into leather. Grooves can be used just for marking lines. For example pulling the groover with light pressure will cut a light line into the leather. Grooves can also be cut deeper, creating a channel in which stitching can be set. Since the final stitched will rest within the groove, below the surface of the leather, they will be less susceptible to abrasions and tearing.

One can also place grooves where they want to create a fold line in the leather material. Or, cut grooves into leather for decorative purposes. For example, adding a groove along either side of a belt. Groovers are generally available as stitching or scratch groovers, each with its potential benefits.

Leather Working Stitching Groover

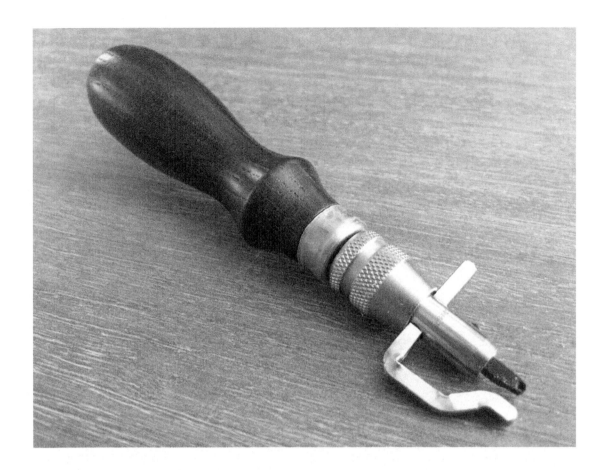

Stitching groovers are generally configured with a grooving tip connected to a wooden handle. Running through the base of the tool near the tip is an edge guide.

The edge guide is a piece of metal that extends and pushes up against the edge of the leather being grooved. It can be adjusted for different widths, then fixed securely in position so it does not move. As the tool is drawn towards you, the edge guide runs along the leather edge, ensuring the groove is at a fixed distance the entire length of the groove.

Since the edge guide is adjustable, multiple grooves can be cut, if desired, into leather creating a wide array of possible design and visually exciting options. With the edge guide removed, the tool can also be used free-hand to make any design one might want in the leather. The leather stitching groover is a very helpful too that you'll likely have in your leather working tool kit.

Leather Working Scratch Groover

A scratch groover is used to cut shallow grooves into leather. Essentially a simplified version of the stitching groover, the scratch groover can be used free-hand to make grooves in leather. They can be used to prepare for stitching, cut decorative grooves, mark light cut lines, or remove leather material at a fold or crease point.

A separate scratch groover is likely not necessary, if you have a stitching groover with a removable edge guide, as without the edge guide, the stitching groover acts just as a scratch groover. If you find you primarily scratch groover, and prefer an array of sizes easily available, one or more scratch groovers might work well for you.

13 - Hardware Fasteners & Setter Tools

Leather hardware and fasteners are used to join pieces of leather together. The types of joining can be temporary, or more permanent depending on the hardware used.

Fasteners can be made of many different types of material. Mostly they are steel, brass, nickel, and copper. Commonly you'll see rivets, snaps, and grommets. Each has it's own main purpose, while they also have variations in aesthetic and cantonal appeal.

Application of fasteners can be done manually with just a few general tools, manually with specialized tools, or mechanically using setting and pressing machines.

A rivet is a two-piece mechanical fastener used to join two pieces of material together. One side of a rivet has a round shaft with a head on the end. The other side, called the "tail" has another head and an area where the round shaft pushes into. Rivers require pressure to be set into place.

When riveting, holes need to be made into the leather where the rivet shaft will push through. The non-shaft head is set onto a base, the shafted head placed through the material, then pounded with a hammer or mallet. The shaft mushes/deforms into the non-shaft head, creating a joined piece that resembles a dumbbell shape. the leather material is now secured between the rivet heads.

Since rivets need to be secured on both ends during the riveting process, special tools are available to help. They are called rivet setters. Rivet setters are usually a combination of 2 pieces. One is a base that the bottom rivet head sits on. the other is a metal bar, about 6" long, shaped to fit over the top rivet. This bar can be struck with a hammer or mallet to "set" the rivets.

Mechanical rivet machines also exist, where instead of setting them with a hammer, they are set by the pull of a handle. Since rivet machines have a fixed range of motion, they can help produce more accurate results than when doing by hand with a hammer.

Snap Setters

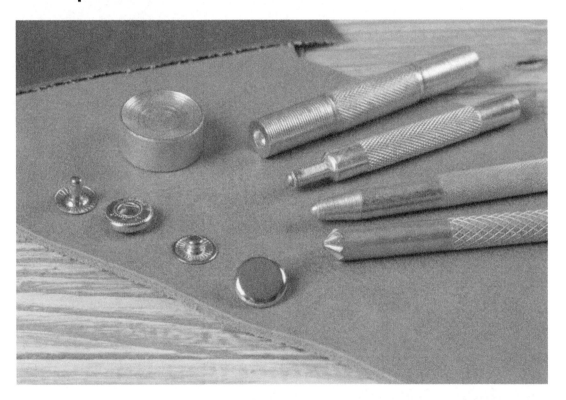

A snap setter is a tool used to set snaps into material. Snaps have generally 5 separate pieces to them (3 on the "top snap" portion, 2 on the "bottom snap" portion). The snap setter is used to align the snap portions to the material, and provide a surface to hit them (with a hammer or mallet) to set them in place. This is performed on one piece of material for the "top snap", and a seaport piece of material for the "bottom snap". When the snaps are "snapped" together, the material is joined.

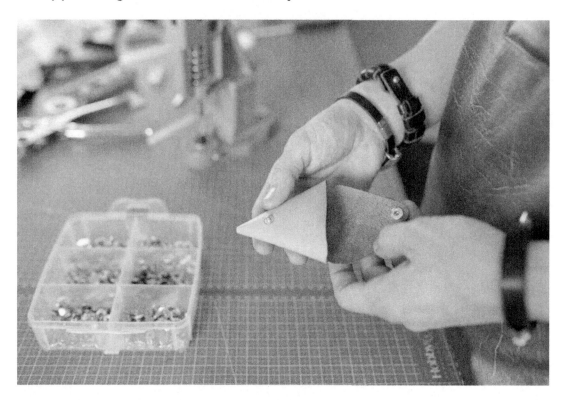

Hand Press Setter Machine

A hand press is a machine that sets snaps, rivets, eyelets, and grommets. While there are manual methods where these hardware types can be applied by hand with some striking force, a mechanized process can lead to much easier, faster application of these hardware pieces.

The hand press machine operates by having a fixed range of motion. It is mechanically connected to a lever arm, that when pressed down by hand, transfers the force through the machine and into the hardware being set (snaps, rivets, grommets, etc.). A hand press can help when you're doing higher volume production or seek to save time and energy over manually setting hardware by striking with hammers, mauls, or mallets.

Foot Press Setter Machine

A foot press is a machine that sets snaps, rivets, eyelets, and grommets. While there are manual methods where these hardware types can be applied by hand with some striking force, having a mechanized process can lead to much easier, and faster application of these construction elements, especially in leather working and fine leather craft.

The foot press machine operates by having a fixed range of motion. It is mechanically connected to a large foot pedal, that when pressed with the feet, transfers the force through the machine and into the hardware being set (snaps, rivets, grommets, etc.). since the foot drives the force, these machines also provide benefit by allowing the hands to be free for holding onto the material being joined. A foot press can help when you're doing higher volume production or seek to have consistent, high-quality results.

Snap Removal Tool (or screwdriver)

Snap removal tools are used to remove snaps that have already been set. Sometimes when working we realize that a snap will need to be undone or moved (from a design change, a snap is damaged, etc.). Snap removal tools are sturdy, metal tools that will disassemble a snap so it can come free from the material it was originally joined to.

Some of these tools are hand-held, and require a fair amount of force to squeeze them. Others are table-mounted, providing a bit more leverage and an easier task of pushing a lever arm to free the snap from the material.

Tack Puller

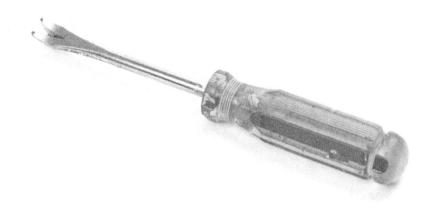

A tack puller is a hand tool generally with a v-slotted metal tip that is used to pry up tacks and nails. It can be used in some cases to help loosen hardware that is attached to leather goods. While a specific removal tool is usually best (snap removal tool, etc.), the general capabilities of a tack puller might come in handy on occasion.

Grommets and Eyelets

Grommets and eyelets are metal hardware that can be applied to leather work to reinforce holes in the leather. For example, if you have a hole where a string or rope will pass through. Over time, the rope's movement will begin to wear down the leather material around the hole, weaken it, and possibly lead to a tear in the material. A grommet or eyelet will cover the inside of the hole, protecting the leather from chaffing caused by the rope.

Grommets and eyelets are available in a wide variety of sizes, colors, and materials. Some common ones include brass, steel, nickel, and copper. Their application can be for both aesthetic and functional reasons.

14 - Holding Tools

Leather holding tools are used to hold leather while it is being worked. For example, one might want to use pliers to hold a leather piece while burnishing it, or applying edge paint. They might be helpful to hold things while stitching, or making a specialized cut. Others hold glued leather pieces securely in place while the leather glue dries. While not primary leather working tools, tools that hold leather can be helpful every now and then for various needs.

It's important to remember that any clamp or pliers that come into contact with the leather should have a soft surface on which it contacts the leather. In not, the leather could get deformed, cut, or marred by uneven surfaces on the clamp/pliers. Some clamp/plier jaws are coated with leather, making them perfect for leather on leather contact during holding activities.

Smooth Jaw Pliers

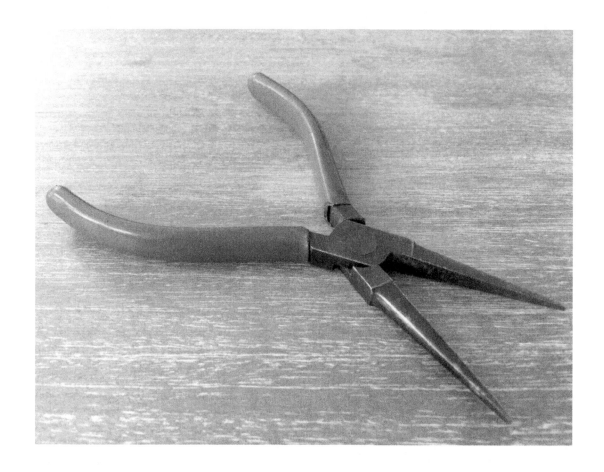

Smooth jaw pliers are a tool with a smooth surface on their "jaws", or contact points. These can be helpful when working with some leathers, as the smooth surface will be less likely to mar the leather surface. You'll need to be aware not to press down too hard as the edges of the jaws can leave an indentation. Though, if used lightly, they can provide a helpful grip during some leather working steps.

Leather Edge Clamp

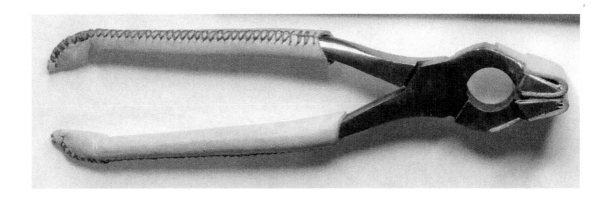

Leather edge clamps are specialty tools that are usually made of steel with rubberized clamp jaws. The jaws are smooth so they don't mar the leather, and the rubber coating makes it even less likely they'll leave any marks. Plus, the rubber coating helps with gripping the leather securely.

Edge clamps are useful for holding glued leather pieces together securely while the glue dries. They can also be used in various instances when holding a piece of leather tightly with one hand is more advantageous using a tool than it is by only a hand.

Some edge clamps are used for flattening leather. Others are made of metal. and yet others are finished with a layer of leather on the flat jaws to ensure a soft and non-marring surface when in contact with leather working pieces.

Cantle Pliers

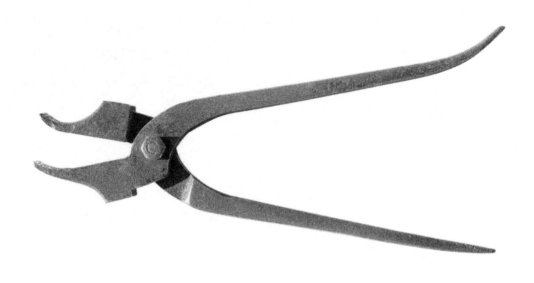

Cantle pliers are a specialized leather working tool that is used mainly for forming leather around the cantle portion of a leather saddle. They are usually metal with smooth jaws that won't leave marks on the leather.Cantle pliers usually come highly polished, in zinc or steel, and are also handy for us in shaping leather handles and similarly functioning leather goods parts.

Curved Jaw Pliers

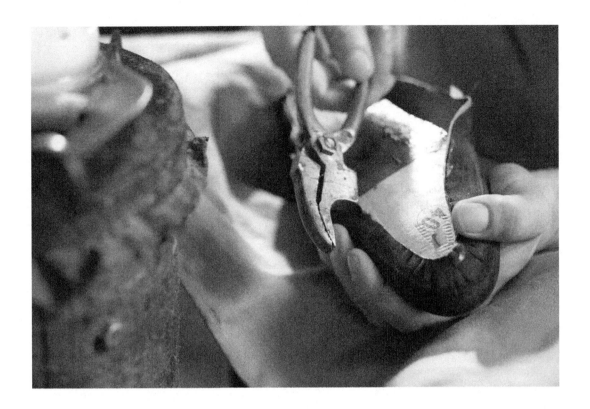

Curved jaw pliers are popular with cobblers, allowing them to firmly grasp leather and bend it/hold it around the edges of shoes and boots during construction. Their shape make this a much more efficient and effective process.

15 - Marking Tools

Much of leather working revolves around cutting and shaping leathers into an amazing final design. To accomplish that, leather marking tools are extremely helpful. They allow us to put marks onto the leather, some temporary and some permanent, that can be useful guides as we cut, trim, punch, and sew.

Across the types of tools, we'll see some that are for scratching, some for pricking, stippling, some for straight lines, some for curved lines and others for corners. Most any leather marking need you might have can benefit from use of the correct, or most helpful, marking tool.

Overstitch Wheel

An overstitch wheel is a tool designed for marking stitch hole locations on leather. It is comprised of a wheel metal with sharp points that go all around it. When rolled onto the leather, the points leave a slight impression in the material. It serves as a perfect guide for pricking or stitching later on.

When you're planning to hand-sew a piece, it's helpful to know exactly where the stitch holes will be. While, one might use pricing irons to make these marks, each time the iron is moves it might not be perfectly aligned with the previous one. An overstitch wheel, if used aligned to a straight-edge, will provide a straight guide of hole marks in a very consistent pattern.

These tools come in various pattern sizes so you can find one that matches the stitch volume you need per inch. A range is certainly preferred as you might want larger spacing on thicker, larger leather pieces. And smaller, narrower spacing on smaller, more fine leather pieces.

Overstitch wheels can also be used after the stitching is complete, to go "over" the "stitches". This gently presses them down, securing them more closely to the leather surface and leading to a more durable and aesthetically pleasing stitch.

Some overstitch wheels come with a "fence". This is an additional metal piece that attaches to the tool, allowing for a variable distance to be set for the wheel to be from the edge of the leather. For example, if you want the stitch line to be 1/4" off the leather's edge, the fence can be set to 1/4" and then wherever the tool is used the markings will be at a consistent distance from the edge.

Pricking Wheel

A pricking wheel is a tool designed for marking stitch hole locations on leather. It is comprised of a wheel metal with very sharp points that go all around it. It is visually similar to an overstitch wheel, though the pricking wheel generally has sharper points that penetrate the leather more deeply.

This can be helpful when hand-stitching smaller items, or of benefit even when planning to use pricking irons to make all of the stitching holes (using the pricked markings as a guide).

Pricking wheels come in various sizes and point spacings so you can choose the one that will best work with the leather craft project's needs.

Some pricking wheels come with a "fence". Th fence is an additional metal piece that attaches to the too, and allows for a variable edge distance to be set. For example, if you want the stitch line to be 1/8" away from the leather's edge, the fence can be set to 1/8". Wherever the tool is used, the wheel markings will be at a consistent distance in from the edge.

Wing Divider/Compass

A wing divider/compass is a tool used to mark the surface of leather, most commonly related to circular or curved lines. Very much like the compass used in mathematical studies, the wing divider has two arms with points on the bottom. They are joined at the top, and in the middle have an adjustable screw with allows for an increase or decrease in distance between the points.

Since it is joined at the top, one point can be placed in a fixed position and the other rotated. The rotated arm will always move around a 360-degree, circular arc, making this a great tool for marking circles, corners, and any kind of curve. As the distance between the arms can be changed, a wide array of circular sizes can be drawn.

Wing dividers/compasses usually have a sharp, metal tips. This allows for precise placement, and also the ability to scratch a line into the leather's surface. For arcs, semi-circles, dividing lines, these are great. If desired and in a pinch, just one arm can be held/used as a scratch awl, for marking leather up.

Leather Working Corner Tool

A leather corner tool is a stencil guide used to mark off corners and small curves on leather material. Often made of plastic, they are helpful in marking off curved areas. If thick enough, they can even be used as a cutting guide right on top of the leather. The knife can carefully trace the curve, ensuring a geometrically accurate and clean, smooth, curved cut.

Leather Stippler

A leather stippler is a tool used mainly for leather carving. It usually has a wooden handle and a metal end with several, pointed tips that generally form a circular pattern. When pressed into the leather, the tips leave a pointed pattern in the material. Pressing can continue, offering a way to add texture to background of leather carving work. If you are looking to add that stippled/pointed look and feel to a carved piece, the leather stippler can be a helpful leather working tool for the kit.

16 - Mauls, Mallets, & Hammers

Mauls, mallets, and hammers are used for a variety of impact tasks during leather working. The choice of which to use is driven by a combination of use and personal preference. Generally, mauls work well for punching and tooling. Mallets can be used with tooling and punching. Hammers work well for forming leather, especially in show making and saddlery.

When choosing a maul, mallet, or hammer, it's important to think about how they'll be used most. The biggest factor in selection is the combination of surfaces – the hitting surface, and the surface being hit.

For example, hitting a metal punch with a metal hammer can damage both the hammer and punch. So for this use a nylon maul or a natural hide mallet (both softer surfaces than metal) would work. Let's explore more about each.

Leather Working Mauls

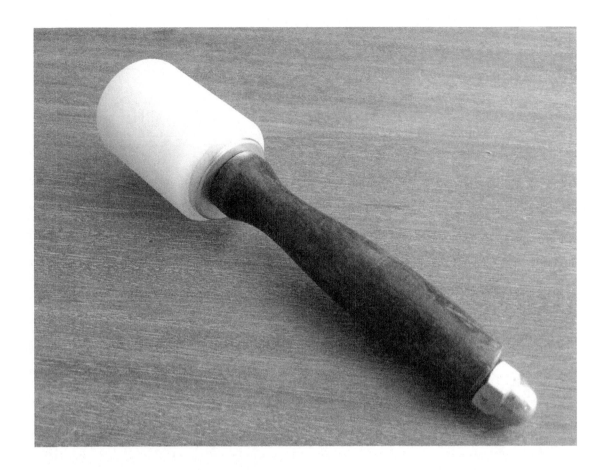

Leather working mauls are hitting tools that have a weighted head wrapped in a nylon cylinder. The softness of the nylon makes it suitable for hitting metal leather working tools, such as punches and stamps. Since the nylon is dense, it provides a very solid and effective hitting surface that absorbs shock and delivers a steady hit. Since it is soft, it won't damage the tools.

Mauls come in different sizes and weights. The heavier mauls will generate more hitting force, though will be a little heavier to hold/swing. It is very much personal preference as to the weight and style of the maul used.

Leather Working Mallets

Leather working mallets are used mainly for striking/hitting other tools. They have a large, cylindrical head and can be made from plastic or raw hide. The raw hide versions usually have a rolled raw hide top, finished so it's very dense while retaining some softness. This helps with shock absorption as well as the softer surface being less likely to damage metal tools when struck. The raw hide mallets are generally more expensive than the plastic versions.

Mallets need to be inspected frequently. With consistent use, the hitting surfaces can begin to show wear, cracks, or even start to chip off. This isn't seen as much with nylon mauls.

Leather Working Tack Hammer

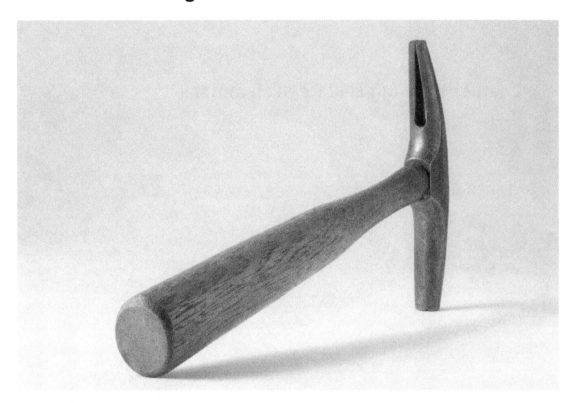

Leather working tack hammers are use frequently in upholstery work. They are thin hammers, usually with steel heads that have two different ends. A "starting" end allows the tacks to be placed and hit to be "started" into the material. This same end can be used, with its grooves, to pull tacks out. The other end has a small, flat hammering surface to hammer the tacks in.

Other versions of tack hammers include those used for saddlery. They also have thin, steel heads and work well for forming leather or performing tack work in difficult-to-reach areas. In this case their small size is an asset. Tack hammers come in maybe subtle variations, each with unique benefits specific to their planned use.

Leather Working Ball Peen Hammer

Leather working ball peen hammers are used mostly for smoothing out or pounding out seams on rawhide. They head is composed of a ball-shaped, rounded end, and a flat, hammering end. The roundness of the ball helps it provide surface pressure to areas and in ways not always possible with the more standard flat end (although it has that too if needed). It can be handy to have if one does a lot of saddle work or sewing of thicker leathers.

Leather Working Rivet Hammer

Leather working rivet hammers are specialized hammers used for rivet setting (securing rivet hardware onto leather material). They have a very well-balanced head that provides ample once in a comfortable way for securing rivets in place. Rivet hammers are not wildly different than other hammers, though the personal preference for a weighted head just for this job might be appealing. For someone that does a lot of riveting by hand, a rivet hammer could be a helpful addition that makes the work easier.

Leather Working Tap-Off Hammer

Leather working tap-off hammers are specialized hammers often used in leather tooling work. They have wide, flat heads made of steel.

Tap-off patterns are decorative leather design templates that can be hammered, or "tapped" into a leather piece. Rather then stamping or engraving similar designs by hand over and over, they can be made into a tap-off pattern.

Once this pattern is made, it can be laid onto a prepared leather surface, and them hammered across it's surface to imprint that tap-off design into the leather below it. Since the entire surface is being hammered, a hammer with a wide, flat surface works great here. Thus, tap-off hammers are a great choice for tap-off work. As an alternative, shoemaker's hammers can be used for tap-off work as well.

Leather Working Saddler's Hammer

Leather working saddler's hammers are used to help form leather and hammer seams. The head is usually made of steel, with long, tapered ends. On end usually has a narrow tip, while the other is often a little wider and rounded. They are great choices when hammering in hard-to-reach places and for lighter hammering work.

Leather Working Shoe Hammer

Leather working shoe hammers are used often for hammering over stitching, tapping through sharp folds, and securing glued leather pieces together. They feature a wide, heavy steel head that produces a deep, steady impact. Used frequently in shoemaking work, they are also a popular choice for those working in saddlery, luggage making, or making bags.

Leather Working Fitting Hammer

Leather working fitting hammers are used mostly for hammering seams and for flattening leather pieces. They look like a hammer head, without a wooden handle. They are made of steel, and the piece in between the two heads is where it is held. One end is generally rectangular, narrow, and flat. The other end usually round, wider, and flat. If one pounds seams often and likes the feel of this handle style over a typical hammer, the fitting hammer might be a helpful leather working tool addition.

17 - Measuring Tools

When working with leather, measuring tools are so helpful in marking everything from cut lines, to punch and pricking marks. They're even used when laying out intricate and decorative designs in leather carving.

Measuring tools come in a wide variety of options, shapes, sizes, and configurations for both general and specialized uses. Let's take a look.

Leather Thickness Gauge

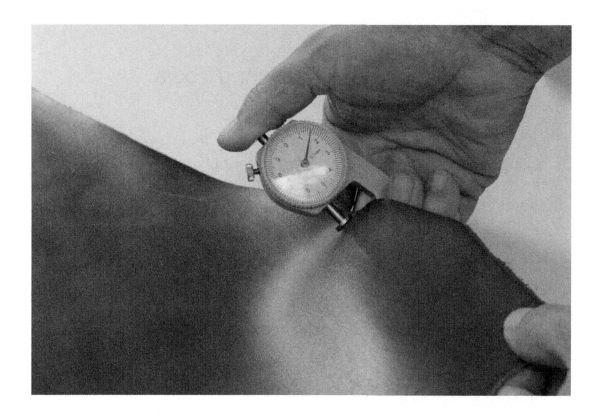

Leather thickness gauges are tools that measure the thickness of leather. Different leather thicknesses are generally used for different products. For example, thinner leathers for wallets, and thicker leathers for bags. It's very helpful to know the general thickness of leather used for any project.

This helps ensure uniformity of the materials used (so the overall feel of the finished product is consistent). It helps when purchasing leather so you know what to buy. It also helps when you're shaving or skiing leather, know know you've reached the goal thickness.

Leather thickness gauges come in a few different forms. Some are flat pieces of wood or plastic with a tapered notch running into it. There are measurements noted along the notch, and depending how far the leather fits into the notch, the corresponding marking will tell it's thickness.

Other leather thickness gauges are in caliper form. The leather is placed into the device and a metal rod is pushed down onto the leather, securing it between two points. Based on how far the rod was pushed down, the leather of the thickness is displayed. Displays can be either analog with a needle layout in analog calipers, or digital with a digital numeric layout in digital calipers.

Common leather thicknesses run from about 1oz (1/64" or .4mm) to 20oz (5/16" or 8mm).

Rulers/Squares

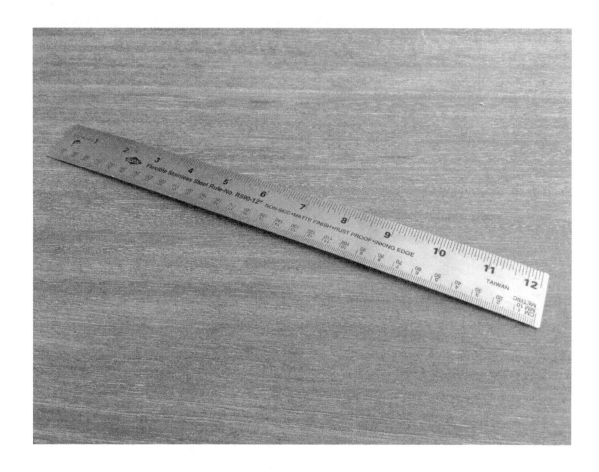

Rulers and squares are used in measuring and cutting leather. They come in many shapes and sizes (some rulers are bendable so even curves can be measured).

One thing to keep in mind when looking at rules and squares is the ability for it to help making leather cuts. Rulers with cork or non-slip bottoms keep them in place on the material being measured. This makes them useful for drawing steady lines, and also serving as a cutting edge when cutting leather.

The cutting blade can simply be run over the material, slightly pressed against the ruler to act as a guide. when used in this way, it's important to ensure the ruler is either thick enough (thicker metal), or raised enough (on a thicker cork bottom, for example) to ensure it provides enough height to keep the blade from jumping off the material and onto the ruler.

Rulers and squares are a very common and useful group of leather working tools.

Leather Working L-Square

Squares, also known as I-squares, are generally an I-shaped ruler. They have a longer ruler-like side, and connected at a 90-degree right angle is another, shorter straight side. This allows for measuring and marking of corners and perpendicular lines, knowing the angle is precise. L-squares are usually available in metal, plastic, or wood materials. They are marked in inches (imperial), millimeters (metric), or any variation of scale and units.

Leather Working Straight Edge Ruler

Rulers are generally straight, approximately 12" – 36" long, and made of metal, wood, or plastic. Measurement markings are either printed or etched along their length and can be in inches (imperial), millimeters (metric), or any variation of scale and units. Some rulers have a metal edge built in to serve as a durable edge for running a pen or pencil against while marking material.

Tape Measure

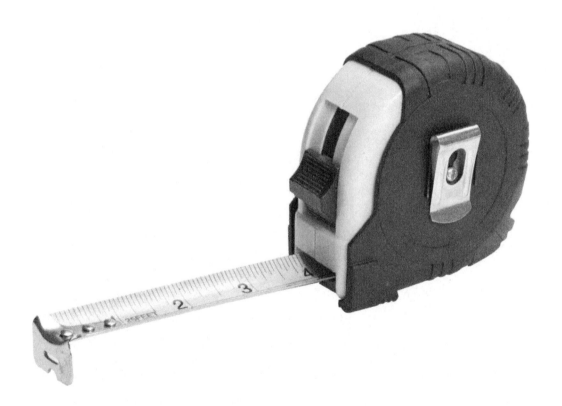

A tape measure is a type of measuring device that often retracts into a rolled case. They are generally made with bendable metal "blade" that has the measurements printed on it. When pulled from the case, the blade extends out and can be held next to or on top of materials to determine their size. Measurement markings can also be made based on the measurements they provide.

When done making measurements, the blade can be retracted back into the case, making for convenient carry and storage. Tape measures are usually available in inches (imperial), millimeters (metric), or any variation of scale and units. They are also available in various lengths, most often ranging from 6' to 25'.

Leather Thickness Sample Set

Leather thickness sample sets are a group of small leather samples groups together and each marked with the specific leather thickness of the sample that it is. Different leather projects require different leather "weights" (thicknesses), it's helpful to know which will work best.

A leather thickness sample may be comprised of 10-20, 3" x 2" pieces of leather of varying thicknesses (weights). They are usually joined with a metal ring, or a string, to neatly keep them all together. Leather thicknesses range from about 1oz (1/64" or .4mm) to 20oz (5/16" or 8mm). Being able to hold, feel, and see the specific thinnesses is quite helpful when deciding what weight material will be most useful for the work.

Measuring Tape

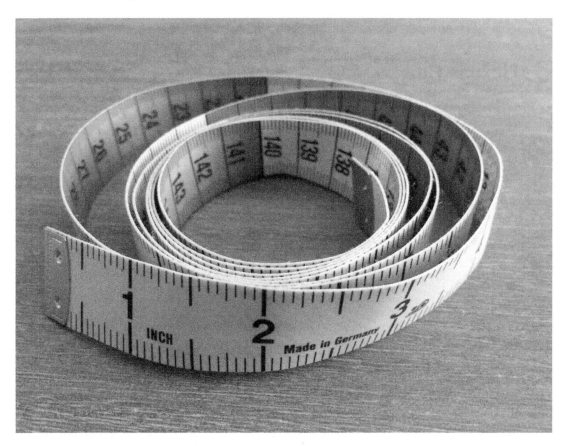

A measuring tape is a type of flexible distance measuring device. It is essentially a ruler printed onto a flexible material, such as plastic. This allows it to easily measure organic curves and shapes, such as people. For example measuring a waist size when making a belt or calf size when crafting leather boots. It is important that the material used does not stretch easily, either new or over time, as the accuracy of it depends on it's ability to provide the correct measurements Measuring tapes are usually available in inches (imperial), millimeters (metric), or any variation of scale and units.

Flexible Ruler

A flexible ruler can be bent and curved, while still providing measurement gradations. This is helpful for planning out and tracing curves and various shapes that benefit from rounded edges and lines.

18 - Moulders

Leather working moulders are metal tools that assist in the moulding of leather. They're generally a handle (either wooden or metal), with a solid metal end that comes out. The metal end is rounded. This allows it to fit into, under, and around many areas.

They can provide a supportive pressure that holds leather in places when it is being hammered or shaped, when moulding leather in either the wet or dry methods.

19 - Pricking Irons

Leather working pricking irons are metal tools with a grouping of equally-spaced "teeth", sharp points arranged in a line. They are used to mark the location of stitching holes onto leather material. Since leather is a generally thick material, holes need to be pre-made for the needle and threads or laces to go through. The holes can then be made using awls or chisels.

Pricking irons are made with a set distance between points. This is in order to ensure the hole marks are a uniform and consistent distance apart. This allows for tight seams and a clean visual appearance on the completed leather piece. Pricking irons are usually only intended for marking leather, not pushing holes through it.

While a pricking iron might push into the leather, leather chisels are more functional and intended for making the actual holes that pricking irons are used to mark off. Pricking irons come in variations of tooth counts, commonly ranging from one to twelve. This allows the leather crafter to choose which will be most helpful.

For example, when pricking a length of leather in a straight line, more teeth will help accomplish this faster. When pricking a curved end in a leather piece, fewer teeth will be more helpful as it allows the crafter to follow the curve of the edge prick by prick.

20   - Chisels

Leather working chisels are metal tools with a grouping of equally-spaced sharp "teeth", sharp points arranged in a line. They are similar in look to pricking irons, though chisels are intended to make the holes in leather, where pricking irons are intended only to mark the holes in leather.

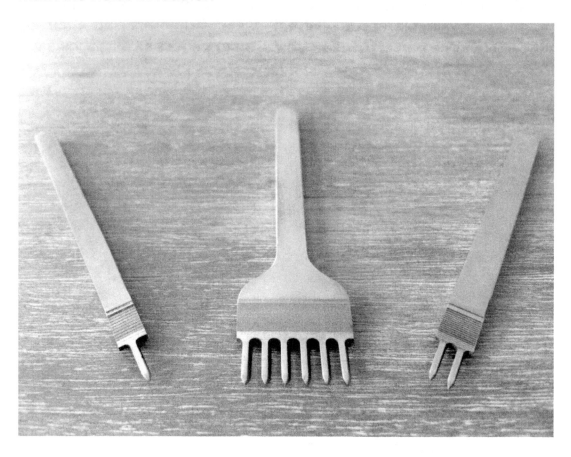

Leather chisels come in variations of tooth counts, commonly ranging from one to twelve. This allows the leather crafter to choose which will be most helpful. For example, when chiseling a length of leather in a straight line, more teeth will help accomplish this faster. When chiseling a curved end in a leather piece, fewer teeth will be more helpful as it allows the crafter to follow the curve of the edge, hole by hole.

Also important on chisels is the shape of the tips of the teeth. The tooth shape directly impacts the look of the hole in the leather, which will influence the overall visual design of the finished piece. Some chisels have angled teeth, some diamond shaped teeth, and others have finer points.

Keeping the leather working chisels well-maintained definitely helps ensure they deliver smooth, clean cuts. They are available in many sizes, so the crafter can choose what works best, from thin, fine leather projects to thicker, heaver leather projects that require larger chisels. These are very common tools that most leather crafters will have in their leather working tool set.

21 - Punch Tools

Leather punches are tools with rounded blades used to cut holes into leather. Generally, the based are sharpened edges around a hollow metal cylinder, perfect for creating a circular hole. The punch blades can be interchangeable allowing a single handle to accommodate many sizes. Or, they can be individual tools where the blade and handle are formed from a solid piece of metal.

Punches need to be strong as they are used by pounding them with force. A piece of leather to be punched is placed on a nylon surface, on top of a hard, sturdy surface (such as granite). The punch lined up and rested on the leather where it will make the hole. Then, a mallet, hammer, or maul is used to strike the top of the punch. The force of the strike pushes the punch through the material. The softer nylon surface protects the punch blade from damage, and the granite absorbs much of the force. The result is a, smooth, clean hole punched into the leather.

Leather punches come in a very wide variety of shapes and sizes for many different uses. It is also important to maintain the blades well, as a sharp blade will produce superior punching results.

Round Strap End Punch

Leather round strap end punches are used for cutting the rounded ends of straps and belts. They work by placing the punch over the end of the leather material that is to be cut, then striking the punch with a mallet, hammer, or maul. The result is a semi-circular cut. Round star end punches come in a variety of sizes so the proper one can be selected based on the project's needs.

English Point Strap End Punch

English point strap end punches are used for cutting the ends of straps and belts. They work by placing the punch over the end of the leather material that is to be cut, then striking the punch with a mallet, hammer, or maul. The result is cut that gradually tapers in from the edges and comes to a soft point at the end. Round star end punches come in a variety of sizes so the proper one can be selected based on the project's needs.

Leather Round Drive Hole Punch

Round drive punches are thin, cylindrical steel tools used to cut holes in leather. The cutting end is made of a sharpened edge around a hollow metal tip. There is usually an opening in the cylinder near the cutting end. The other end of drive punches is solid steel.

A round drive punch is set onto the leather it will cut, then hit or "driven" with a hammer, mallet, or maul. The force generated but the hit drives the cutting end through the leather. This creates a hole in the leather and a small leather circular piece that used to fill what is now the hole.

As more holes are punched, the circular pieces begin to push up through the cylinder and out of the opening near the cylinder end. Alternatively, after a few punches, the excess circular pieces can be pushed down and out of the punch with a small pin or other thin implement, pushed through the opening.

Round drive punches are available is many different hole sizes. Some are individual tools fixed in size. Others are handles with interchangeable punch size tips, requiring less storage space, though some additional time to change tips between sizes. Most leather crafters will find themselves with at least a few round drive punches in their leather working tool kit.

Round punches are great for making buckle holes in belts, as well as across leather projects when creating holes for grommets, eyelets, or even holes for large laces.

Leather Trace Punch

Leather trace punches are metal tools with a cutting edge used to punch tapered holes into leather. If you imagine an oblong cut, with one side wider than the other, that is what a trace punch creates. They are generally made of steel with highly-sharpened blades.

Trace punches are most popular for harness work, though can be useful for a variety of cutting/punching needs based on their unique shape. Multiple sizes are available for use based on preference and what might work best for your project.

Leather Oval Punch

Leather oval punches are metal tools with a cutting edge used to create oval-shaped holes in leather material. There often have an opening in the punch near the cutting end. The other end is usually made of solid steel, providing an area to be struck with a hammer, mallet, or maul.

Oval punches come in a variety of sizes, offering many options to ensure the crafter has the size that is most helpful the the type of project and work that they are doing.

Leather Rotary Punch

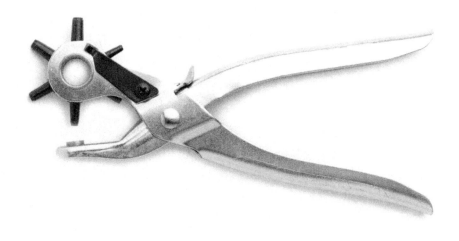

Leather rotary punches are manually operated, hand-held metal tools with multiple hole-sized punches used to make holes in leather material. The punches are usually arranged around a rotatable, circular "turret". There is often an integrated surface for the punches to much onto when cutting.

They work by rotating the turret to select the side punch to use, placing the leather material between the punch and cutting surface, then squeezing the grips closed by hand. The gripping motion pushes the punch through the leather and results in a hole.

Rotary punches are available with different sized punches. Some have interchangeable punches, making it easy to have any 6 or so available at a time, quickly accessible at the spin of a turret and squeeze of the grip.

Individual punches usually yield more precise results, and also allow more force to be used resulting in generally smoother, cleaner cuts. Though, for smaller holes and thinner leathers, rotary punches can be a quite effective leather working tool.

Leather Button Hole Punch

Button hole punches are metal tools used to simultaneously cut holes and a connected slit, into leather material. When working with button studs, they join leather by pushing through a hole that is slightly smaller than the stud. Hence, once through, the stud holds the button in place.

I order to have enough room to push through, there needs to be extra flexibility around the hole to accommodate the stud. This is done by cutting a slit directly connected to the button hole. The slit parts the leather, making it flexible enough around the hole to accommodate the larger stud.

Button holes can be made using a standard round drive punch, then cutting a slit below it with a knife. Alternatively, they be made with a button hole punch. This makes it much easier, with more consistent results, as all of the cutting is done with one tap of a mallet, hammer, or maul onto the button hole punch.

They are available is different sizes so the proper size can be selected based on the needed sizes of the hole and the button stud hardware that will be used.

Leather Slot Hole Punch

Leather slot hole punches are metal tools with a cutting edge used to create narrow, oblong holes in leather material. There is usually an opening in the punch near the cutting end to insert a thin metal wire and push to release the cut leather material. The other end is usually made of solid steel, providing an area to be struck with a hammer, mallet, or maul.

Slot hole punches are helpful when making holes to run straps through, such as in bag or case making work.

Leather Corner Punch

Leather corner punches are metal tools with sharp, rounded edges used to cut through leather. Corners on leather projects can be cut by hand, which requires measuring, then carefully cutting out the curved shape. Alternatively, using a corner punch makes this much easier. The corner shape is set as a metal blade and can simply be placed onto the material and hit with a mallet, hammer, or maul to make the cut.

Corner punches are available in different sizes so one can be found that matches the crafter's need. If there are preferences for more rounded, or more angled corners, different diameters are available as well. If you're cutting many similarly-sized piece with rounded corners by hand, these punches can definitely a valuable addition to your tool set.

Leather Shaped Hole Punches

Leather shaped hole punches are metal tools with share edges used to cut holes in leather. The cutting edges are available many different shapes, making it easy to add decorative or functional cuts into leather material. An example of the shapes available include stars, diamonds, hearts, squares, and semi-circles.

Cutting intricate shapes by hand can take time. Cutting these with a shaped hole punch make it a much easier, and more efficient process. These punches are usually made of steel with one end the sharpened cutting blade, and the other solid steel. The solid end us

179

used for hitting with a hammer, mallet, or maul to generate the force that drives the punch through the leather.

If you do much decorative leather work or plan to cut out many versions of a specific decorative shape, a shaped hole punch could be a valuable tool to have.

Leather Stitching Punch

A leather stitching punch is a metal tool with a group of round punches grouped in a straight line. When making holes along a leather's edge that will be used for running leather lacing through, it is helpful to have the holes both be a consistent size, and a consistent distance between each other.

If this is done with a standard hole punch, each hole need to be measured, lined up, and punched. A stitching punch makes this much easier as hitting it once will punch several holes into the leather at the same time. Stitching punches might have 3, 5, or more blades.

The size of the holes and number of blades available varies, so the crafter can choose one or more stitching punches that would help most for their particular project.

Hand Sewing Punch

A leather hand sewing punch is used to punch small, round holes into leather. They are usually made of stainless steel, with two grips, a punching surface, and a punch tip. The punching surface is generally circular shaped and rotatable, with about 6 differently-sized holes of differing sizes.

When using it, the preferred hole size can be rotated under the top, and the leather laid onto the punch surface. The handles are then squeezed together, pushing the punch tip down into the selected hole size, and a hole is cut into the leather.

This is another style of hole punch, and can be a quick way to put clean holes into thinner leathers.

Leather Ventilator Punch

A leather ventilator punch is a metal tool that punches a group of round holes into leather material. They have a solid steel hitting end, and a cutting end with several, usually about 6, small, round punches mounted in a generally circular pattern.

Ventilator punches make it easy to punch multiple small, grouped holes in leather goods where air flow can be helpful. This is often seen in bags and cases where air flow can be helpful, and sometimes shoes.

If you're looking for a ventilator punch it's likely for a particular project, so ensure the hole size and cut pattern will match your needs. If so, these can surely help save time over manually measuring and punching individual holes.

Leather Rosette/Concho Cutter

A rosette cutter, sometimes referred to as a concho cutter is a type of metal punch that cuts rosette shapes out of leather. Rosettes are decorate embellishments applied to leather work, usually saddlery. They can come in different designs, though the most common is a circle with about 16 rounded points that make up the perimeter. Think a many-pointed star, though with rounded points.

Cutting these each by hand can become very time consuming. With a rosette cutter, it is much faster. Just place the cutter on the leather, hit it with a hammer, maul, or mallet, and the rosette is cut. Many can be made in a fraction of the time of manually-cut pieces. These tools come in various sizes, each of which can be used depending on your needs.

Leather Rotary Punch Machine

A leather rotary punch machine is a table-mounted machine that helps punch holes into leather material. Whereas manual punches are most common, for those looking for ease of use, consistency of results, and mechanically-assisted punching, the rotary punch is available.

They generally have a solid punching surface where the leather can rest. Above is the punch arm that is controlled by a manually-operated, rotating wheel. Offset guides can be set to ensure consistent distance of the holes from the edge of the material, such as when making holes in belts.

The punch holes in punch machines are often self-centering, making it easy to ensure a proper cut. The distance, center-to-center, between holes is adjustable, as is the tube size for the punch cutters.

These machines are generally very heavy, and do take up table space. If you find yourself doing high-volume or repetitive round hole punching, this could be a useful tool.

Leather Self-Centering Punch Machine

A self-centering punch machine is a table-mounted machine that helps punch holes into leather material. It is very similar to a rotary punch machine, having a solid punching surface where the leather can rest. Above is the punch arm that is controlled by a manually-operated lever that helps apply force that pushes the punch through the leather.

They generally have many punch dies available in different sizes, shaped to cut points, holes, and slots into leather mater of varying thicknesses. The tool is self-centering, helping to provide consistent and accurate cutting results.

Punch machines are generally very heavy, and do take up a fair amount table space. If you find yourself doing high-volume production or repetitive hole punching work for, this could be a useful tool.

22 - Sewing Tools

Leather sewing tools are comprised of a wide range of items used for stitching leather. they generally include needles, thread, sewing machines, and tools to hold leather while you sew. Within these groups there is a great depth of options available that fit across needs, styles, preferences.

While leather can be joined by hardware such as rivets and grommets, sewing provides for a wealth of functional and aesthetic means by which to join leather material together. Leather sewing tools are used to make endless leather goods including wallets, bags, belts, clothing, and shoes.

Leather Sewing Needle

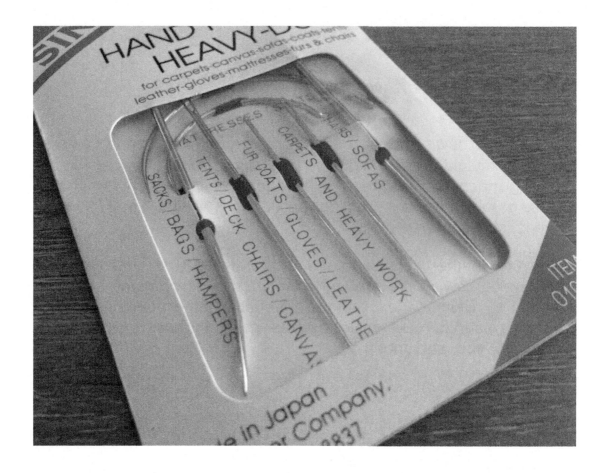

A leather sewing needle is a narrow, cylindrical piece of steel with a sharp point on one end and a small opening, or "eye" on the other. Thread is secured through the eye, and the sharp point of the needle is pushed through material. As the needle goes through the material it pulls the thread. As this is repeated along the edge of leather pieces, resulting in a line of "stitches", the thread binds the leather pieces together.

Sewing needles have been used for over 40,000 years. Today, they come in a wide assortment of options. There are leather-specific needles that have wider points to help pierce thick leathers. There are curved needles (they have a semi-circular, half-moon shape) that make it easier to push through thicker materials such as leather and canvas. Very small needles make it easier to sew smaller, thinners leathers while leaving a smaller hole.

There are also needles for powered sewing machines, each with unique sizes and performance characteristics based on the intended use. A sewing needed, either hand-needle or one used in a sewing machine, will likely be something a leather worker comes across during their leather craft experience.

Leather Two-Prong Lacing Needle

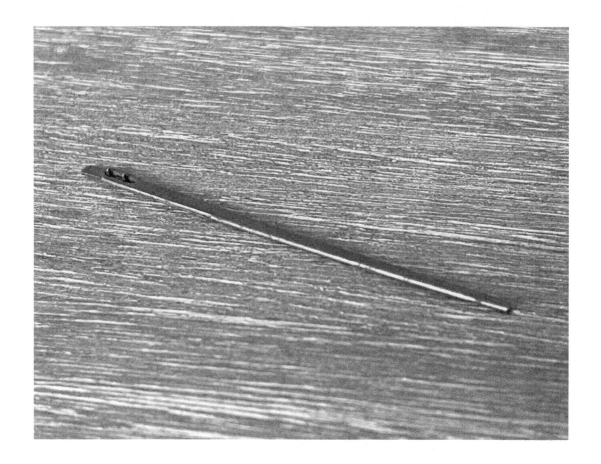

Two-prong lacing needles are a type of hand-sewing needle with two prongs that are used for sewing with leather lace. Typical needles have an eye where thread is passed through and secured. This can be tricky or impossible with some leather laces, and the lace, once tied into a knot by the needle eye, would b too large to pass through the lacing hole in the leather.

Two-prong lacing needed have two prongs under spring tension instead of an eye. The prongs are separated and the lacing material slid between them. When released, the tension between the prongs holds the lace flat, and in place. This helps it maintain a thinner profile when passed through the stitching holes, especially diagonal ones.

These needles are usually made of metal, and are valuable great tool for hand-sewing with leather lace.

Leather Saddler's Harness Needle

Saddler's harness needles are a specialized sewing needle with a blunt tip and strong eyelets. Since leather can be a thick, and tough material, these needles help guide thread through without marking up the leather, and while being sturdy enough to hold up.

Common varieties of needles might also break at the eye when used with thicker threads and through tougher materials. The eye is a thinner part of the metal, and susceptible to breakage. Saddler's harness needed are stronger all around, including at the eyelets.

Often used for saddlery, they can also be used for bag making, shoe making, and any leather work that requires sewing with thick thread through thick material.

Leather Sewing Machine

A leather sewing machine is a powered, mechanical tool used to join materials together via stitches. Stitches are connecting points made between materials by singular strands of fibers or threads. Whereas hand sewing involves carefully making each stitch one-by one, machine sewing allows for much faster, automated stitching.

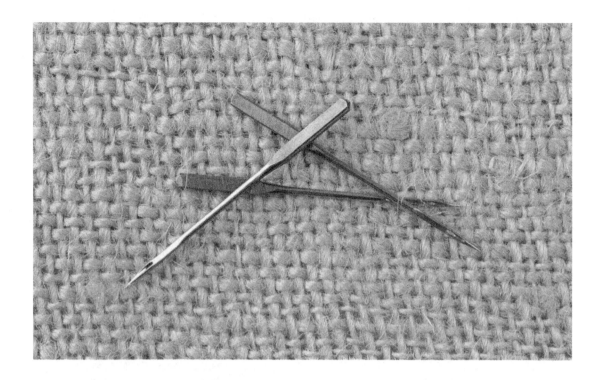

Sewing machines, at a high level, have spools of thread, a sewing surface, a needle, a power source, and a control pedal. The materials to be sewn are guided under the needle, and when the control pedal is pressed, the needle moves up and down, inserting stitches into the material. As this happens, the material is moved through the machine and stitches continuously in a linear fashion. The result is a row of stitching that is clean, consistent, and strong. If a leather crafter is producing a volume of items, or looking for a consistent finish to their products, sewing machines are indispensable tools.

Also since they are powered tools, the amount of human effort needed to continually press a needle through thick thread is greatly minimized. What might have taken hours by hand, might take only minutes by machine.

There are many machine options available. Important considerations when choosing a machine include knowing how heavy the material is that will be sewn, and how durable the machine is. A sturdy, well-maintained machine can last decades or longer.

Leather Stitching Pony

A stitching stitching pony is a wooden tool with two arms used to hold leather items securely while they are being hand-sewn. Leather can be a thick, tough material. Sometimes, having two hands free makes feeding a needle and pulling thread through a much easier process. They are similar to a stitching horse, though much smaller.

The stitching pony is generally placed on a chair, and sat on. It's position is secured by the weight of the person sitting on it, and two vertical arms that extend up that will hold the leather. They're joined in the middle with an adjustment screw, so the space between them can be widened and narrowed. The leather to be sewn is placed in between the arms, and the arms are tightened, holding the leather in place.

It is always important to ensure that any material that touches leather during the leather working process is soft, and won't leave any unwanted imprints or marks behind. Since it's made of smoothed wood, the stitching pony provides a gentle surface for gripping leather. If preferred, something soft such as a cloth or other leather can be placed between the stitching pony arms and the leather being worked, further providing protection from scratches.

For leather crafters that hand-sew often, a stitching pony can be a helpful leather working tool.

Leather Stitching Horse

A stitching horse is a wooden tool with two arms used to hold leather items securely while they are being hand-sewn. Having two hands free makes feeding a needle and pulling thread through leather a much easier process. They are similar to a stitching pony, though much larger.

The stitching horse generally stands on the floor, and includes a seat for a person to sit on. Two large, vertical arms that extend up, and can accommodate very large and thick leather items. They're joined in the middle with an adjustment screw, so the space between them can be widened and narrowed. The leather to be sewn is placed in between the arms, and the arms are tightened, holding the leather in place.

Stitching horses generally feature smooth, wooden surfaces on the arms which protects the leather. It is important that any working surface that comes into contact with leather is soft/smooth, and will not leave unwanted marks or scratches on the material being worked. For additional protection, a soft material can be placed between the arms and the leather being worked, such as soft fabric or even other leather.

For those working on larger leather pieces that require heavy sewing by hand, a stitching horse could be a help addition to the leather working shop.

Leather Table Stitching Clamp

197

A leather table stitching clamp is a wooden tool with two arms used to hold leather securely while it is being hand-stitched. They're joined in the middle with an adjustment screw that can make the space between the arms wider or narrower, ensuring a tight hold around the specific leather being worked on.

It works similarly to a stitching horse or stitching pony, though rather than being sat on, this simply clamps to a table or other work surface.

Leather Stitching Clam

A stitching clam is a wooden tool with two arms used to hold materials, especially leather, securely while it is being hand-stitched. They're joined in the middle with an adjustment screw that can make the space between the arms wider or narrower, ensuring a tight hold around the specific leather being worked on.

while similar to stitching ponies and stitching horses, the stitching clam is a little more simple and just slides under one leg for support. It's position can be adjusted for the proper angle of stitch access, as well and personal comfort. If one does a fair amount of hand-stitching, with smaller to medium-sized leather pieces, a stitching clam might be a help.

Leather Sewing Tower

A leather sewing tower is a wooden tool used to hold leather pieces while being sewn by hand. It is often helpful to have both free hands for stitching work, and a leather sewing tower helps makes that possible by providing a versatile group of holding clamps and surfaces on which to secure leather pieces for stitching.

They are generally secured to a table top. Extending out (about 9"-12") is an arm, onto which two additional arms run, with screws to adjust their distance. Leather can be clamped between each of these arms and the main extension. The main extension can even be position higher or lower on the device.

The flexibility of positions and the shape of the main extension allow for leather to be positioned securely for a number of stitching needs including right-angle stitching. They are similar in function to stitching horses and stitching ponies, For those that do a lot of leather stitching and might prefer the feel of a sewing tower, it's certainly another option to add to the leather craft tools list.

Leather Working Thread

Leather sewing thread is a type of thin yarn, used for joining leather materials together. Threads are very common leather working tools and come in need endless colors. They also come in various "weights", or thicknesses, each with benefits depending on the type of leather being sewn.

Generally, thinner leathers will use lighter "weight", thinner threads. Thicker leathers will usually be sewn with thicker, or heavier "weight" threads. Thread weight choice can be a matter of function. For example, is it strong enough to hold the materials together and not wear out easily from rubbing or abrasions? Thread can also be selected based on aesthetic preference. For example, does the color look great on the leather it is used with? Does the seam size create a nice, finished visual appearance.

Along with colors and wights, threads are also available many different material types. So much thread! Each material type have unique properties that can make it beneficial for some types of leather work over others. Let's see a little more about each and which you might want to add to your leather craft tools list.

Waxed Thread for Leather Working

Waxed thread is a type of thread that is lightly coated in wax. The wax stiffens the thread, making it stronger. This also enables the thread to be more abrasion resistant, water resistant, and stretch less over time.

Waxed threads are great for leather working as the provide a very durable thread that handles well and looks great. Ideal for hand-sewing, these threads are available in a range of colors and thicknesses (weights).

Bonded Nylon Thread for Leather Working

Bonded nylon (or polyester) threads are a very strong, synthetic thread. Whereas many threads are composed of material strands twisted together, bonded nylon is also physically bonded together. This makes it a much stronger thread. The properties of it being nylon (essentially, plastic), make it very sturdy, water resistant, wear resistant, and last a very long time.

For many leather working projects, bonded thread is a staple thread used. They are available in a range of colors and thicknesses, so one can be selected to best suit the project you are working on.

Nylon threads are also great for machine sewing and hand sewing as well.

Linen Thread for Leather Working

Linen thread is made of natural, cotton fibers. While not as strong as waxed or bonded nylon threads, it still provides solid holding strength for thinner leathers and leather goods that will not experience a lot of daily wear.

While functional, linen thread can also be decorative in the color selections chosen. Also, since it is a natural fiber, the look of line thread is certainly a bit different on finished leather goods. If you're working with fine leather accessories or want to try a different visual finish, line thread might be worth added to the leather craft tool list.

Linen thread is generally best for hand sewing, though can be used in lighter machine sewing applications as well.

Sewing Thimble

A thimble is a protective device that fits over a finger, and used to assist in pushing a needle through materials when sewing by hand. they can me made of many different materials including metals, woods, leathers, and plastics.

When sewing by hand, the needle needs to be pushed through the materials being sewn. Certainly with some thicker leathers, this can require a fair amount of force. That force, applied from a finger onto a tiny needle head could be painful or in some cases dangerous, especially over time with repeated stitching.

A thimble covers the finger and provides a harder surface for pushing the needle. So smart! Thimbles are available in different sizes, and different surface finishes/styles, so one can be found that works best with the types of needles and style of sewing being performed. Most leather workers that hand-sew will have one, two, or many needs around the workshop.

Leather Lacing Fid

A leather lacing fid is a metal tool with a pointed end used to stretch and enlarge lacing holes when working with leather. They commonly have a wooden handle for comfortable holding.

It's preferable to have a tight-fitting stitch and appropriately-sized lacing holes on finished leather goods. Depending on the tools available, a leather crafter might find they need to slightly enlarge or adjust some lacing holes, and in those cases a lacing fid can come in handy.

Hand Sewing Punch

A leather hand sewing punch is used to punch small, round holes into leather. They are usually made of stainless steel, with two grips, a punching surface, and a punch tip. The punching surface is generally circular shaped and rotatable, with about 6 differently-sized holes of differing sizes.

When using it, the preferred hole size can be rotated under the top, and the leather laid onto the punch surface. The handles are then squeezed together, pushing the punch tip down into the selected hole size, and a hole is cut into the leather.

This is another style of hole punch, and can be a quick way to put clean holes into thinner leathers.

Wood Burning Tool (also used as a Thread Trimming tool)

A wood burning tool is an electrically-powered tool that is used to burn marks into wood. They generally have a handle, and a metal extension that gets very hot, powered by electricity. When the metal tip is hot, it can be used to burn marks into woods.

This same tool can be used to trim threads, especially nylon and synthetic threads. When sewing by hand, sometimes little pieces of thread are left over after finished the stitch and tying it off. In order to create a visually smooth, and clean finish, the thread can be snipped.

Since scissors can only get so close to the seam, due to the natural material thickness of the scissors, sometimes a little bit of thread fray is left behind. Burning it with a wood burning/thread trimming tool is a very easy way to get rid of these tiny bits of thread.

Just hold the tool lightly on the thread for a very short period of time, and it will burn away. Leather crafters have different preferences for finishing threads, for some, this the leather craft tool of choice.

Hand Held Lighter

When sewing by hand, sometimes when the stitch is finished there is a little bit of thread left behind. Even after trimming with scissors, there remains just a bit of thread fray. Since the scissors have a material thickness to themselves, they can't always get precisely close.

Burning the remaining bits of thread away is a practice some leather workers perform, and a common hand-held, or disposable lighter can work great. Certainly, ensure safe handling practices. When done correctly, this can be an inexpensive and effective way to finish thread trimming on leather goods.

23 - Skiver Tools

Skivers are tools used to remove thin layers of leather material. They generally have a very sharp cutting blade. When the blade is drawn against the leather grain with some pressure applied down upon it, the blade cuts through the leather as it moves along, shaving off a thin layer.

Skiving is helpful In many facets of leather work. It is used, for example when making belts. At the point where the leather is folded over to secure the buckle, there would be double the leather thickness since the material is folder over. This could be bulkier than necessary, as well as potentially uncomfortable to wear. Skiving can be used to thin out the leather, on both sides around the fold, so that when they are joined together it is only about one layer thick. This will look cleaner and wear more comfortably.

This same process can be applied to bag straps, saddlery, and any leather work that involves folding and joining thinker pieces of leather. Skivers are available in hand-held versions, manually drawn against the leather. Skivers are also available in tabletop versions, where the leather is pulled through the skiver.

Additionally, there are skipping knives, used to free-hand skive. Carefully removing leather layers is part art and part skill. Most leather craftsman will at some point have one or several skivers on their leather craft tools list.

Leather Hand Skiver

Leather hand skivers are manually-operated tools for removing thin layers of leather material. They have very sharp blades that are usually either flat, or slightly curved. Skivers are drawn across leather, with downward pressure applied. They shave off a thin layer of leather as they are drawn.

Flat bladed will shave leather in an even way. Curved skiver blades will shave more towards the center of the blade, since that can cut deepest into the material. Curved blades work well for skiving out curved recesses, or for finely controlling the cutting depth but utilizing the narrower blade heights towards the edges of the curved blades.

Hand skiving is effective, though requires practice to produce a consistent result. As each pass is performed manually, the process can yield natural variations.

Leather Tabletop Skivers

Leather tabletop skivers are table-mounted tools used to skiver leather efficiently and with consistent results. They usually come with large 6" – 10" blades, and have adjustable skiing heights.

To skiver with a tabletop skiver, the preferred skiving height is set, leather is placed under the blade, and a lever is lowered to secure the leather in place. Once in place, the leather is pulled through the skiver. This results in a skived piece that matches the height originally set on the skiver.

The thickness of the skive can also be manually adjusted by pushing or pulling on the lever as the leather is being pulled through. This allows for variable thicknesses of the skive, for example towards the ends of a belt or for bag strap.

The incredible benefits of these tools is that it produces a very consistent result, very quickly. What could take hours by hand with a hand skiver can take minutes or seconds with a tabletop skiver. There are few moving parts, and blades can usually be sharpened, making these a leather working tool that can easily see years or decades of use.

Leather Skiving Knives

A leather skiving knife is a speciality knife used to shave off thin layers of leather material. They are usually shaped with a handle, and have a rectangular blade that is sharpened on the short end. This is used for pushing into the leather to shave it away.

The blades are generally available as flat ends, or angled, each with options that include beveled blades for increased control over the thickness of the skiver material. These angle-bladed skiing knives are generally referred to as "lap" skiving knives.

Since these skiving knives are manually operated, they require development of skill to use effectively. Once experienced with their use, skiing knives can quickly remove leather on belts and straps and other work. They also are agile enough to use on smaller pieces and even help with detailed skiving in tight places.

24 - Splitter Tools

Leather splitters are tools used to uniformly remove a thickness of leather material. It can be used to split leather evenly, or split it by a preferred and set thickness. They are comprised of strong, metal blades generally 6" – 8" wide.

Once the thickness of the cut has been set (via an adjustment mechanism), the leather is placed into the splitter, secured by lowering a level, then pulled through. It is split as it is pulled through. This produces clean, and consistent results very quickly.

The thickness of the split can also be manually adjusted by pushing or pulling on the lever as the leather is being pulled through. This allows for variable thicknesses to be split, for example towards the ends of a belt. These can be very useful tools for a leather craftsman who produces higher volume work that required consistent adjustments to leather thicknesses.

25 - Stamping Tools

Leather stamps are metals tools used to imprint decorative designs into leather. They generally have etched designs on the end of a solid metal handle. When rested on the leather and struck with a hammer, mallet, or maul, the force pushes the stamp into the leather material. This leaves an imprint into the leather, of the design that was etched onto the stamp.

Leather stamping is done extensively in the leather tooling craft. Stamps are available in a tremendous variety of shapes, sizes, letters, numbers, and designs. since they only require a striking force, it is a very quick way to add visual embellishments to leather work. Carving the same designs by hand could take hours, with sometimes less-than desirable results.

Stamps are available individually, or in sets. This is an area of leather craft where the imagine can really run wild with imagination and options for using and combing stamps into a decoratively finished piece.

26 - Tooling, Etching, & Engraving Tools

Leather tooling, etching, and engraving are styles of leather working that involve altering the surface of leather material for visual and aesthetic enjoyment. Some of this work involves tremendous skill and practice to do it well.

Leather tooling is the practice of imprinting designs into leather, usually with metal stamps. The stamps available cover a near endless amount of designs, shaped, sizes, letters, and numbers.

Leather etching, which can also involve leather engraving, is the practice of cutting into the leather's surface to produce intricate or decorative patterns. This usually involves the use of specialized knives as the crafters tool for this impressive style of leather work.

Leather Tooling Stylus

A leather tooling stylus is a metal tool with a rounded tip used for tracking patterns into leather for tooling. When a leather crafter has a design in mind and sketched onto leather tracing paper, they can transfer that outline to the leather by pressing into it with the rounded end of a tooling stylus. The pressure applied to the stylus pushes the tracing paper which leaves a colored mark/line in the leather's surface. Those lines traced with the stylus serve as a guide for the next step in the tooling process. These are a handy tool for leather tooling work.

Leather Stippler

The leather stippler, with several sharp, pointed ends, allows for easy texturizing and dot-patterning into the leather surface.

Leather Tracing Film

Leather tracing film is used to help transfer a pencil-sketched design onto leather. The original design, possibly sketched onto a piece of usual paper, can be traced onto the tracing film. When transferring the design to leather, the leather would be moistened, then the tracing film with the design laid over it.

Finally, a leather tooling stylus is used to trace of the tracing film, which transfers an outline of the design pressed into it by the tooling stylus. This is quite a helpful tool for transferring sketches and artwork to leather.

Leather Modeling Spoon

A leather modeling spoon is a tool with a small, spoon-shaped metal end used to remove material from leather. It is generally used for figure carving, where removing leather material is similar to sculpting. The rounded end of the spoon can also be used to smooth out areas of the leather during tooling and etching.

Leather Pyrography Tool

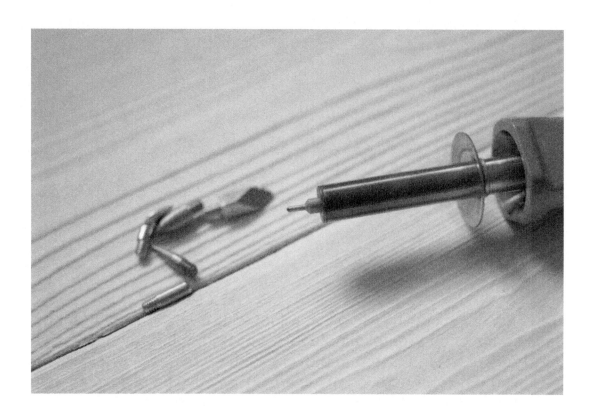

A leather pyrography tool is an electric, pen-shaped device used to burn marks into leather. It usually consists of a handle, with a metal piece that sticks out with a connection point for a burning tip. The tips are interchangeable.

When the pyrography tool is plugged in, the tip heats up. Once hot, it can be used to burn different lines, shapes, patterns, and designs into leather. With a variety of tips available, it makes it very easy to burn patterns, shapes, and even calligraphy into leather.

Leather Engraving Machine

A leather engraving machine allows for automated engraving of leather items, usually from a computer-driven program and interface. They can be help to create consistent, precise engravings across many pieces and items.

27 - Tools Maintenance

Leather working tool maintenance is key to ensuring quality leather working product. When cutting blades are kept sharp, work surfaces clean, and machines well-maintained, they all perform to their best potential.

While it might seem like an afterthought compared to doing fun project (which, yes, are more fun than maintenance :)), in the end great tools will help make great work.

Leather Strop

A leather strop is a tool used in sharpening blades. It helps even out any tiny burrs on the blade edge, making it smooth and sharp. When blades get dull, it is generally due to tiny degradations in quality from the sharpened blade. These can include small nicks and burrs in the cutting edge.

When blades are sharpened, they are usually done so by going over the edge with increasingly-fine-grained stones or sharpeners. Coarser sharpening stones are used first to even out larger burrs. Then finer stones to reduce smaller burrs. Once the leather strop is used, it's usually the last and finest-grained tool in the sharpening lineup.

They help produce a smooth edge to the blade while polishing it some as well. When sharpening knives, a leather strop can be a help addition to the process.

Aluminum Oxide

Aluminum oxide is a chemical compound of aluminum and oxide that is applied to leather stops to aid in the knife sharpening process.

When this compound is rubbed into the leather strop, it help draw a smoother, sharper edge then when stropping with leather alone.

Jeweler's Rouge

Jeweler's rouge is a compound that can be rubbed onto the flesh side of a piece of leather to turn it into an effective polishing strop. The strop can be used when sharpening and polishing knives and edged tools. It helps ensure they are well-maintained for maximum effectiveness when used.

Sharpening Stone

Sharpening stones are solid blocks of material used to sharpen the edges of knives and tools. They come in a wide variety of synthetic, chemical, and natural compositions. Sizes and shapes can vary as well.

The sharpening stones are run in a linear fashion over the edge of the blade being sharpened. This helps to smooth out the blade and reduce any burrs that might have be cause from use. These stones are a common tool used in the sharpening process.

Sharpening Compound

    Sharpening compounds are finely abrasive mixture of natural and or chemical materials used to refine the sharpened edge of knives and blades. The components in sharpening compounds are abrasives intended to polish the blades, and be the last step in the sharpening process.

If one is looking to bring an almost-new edge to a knife or bladed tool, adding sharpening compound onto a strop and running the blade over it can be quite helpful.

28 - Working Surfaces

Leather working surfaces encompass the various work spaces and areas used for leather working. They can include tables, mats, stone slabs, and a number of other various materials and surfaces that help when crafting, tooling, or adding hardware to leather.

Leather craft doesn't require too many surfaces, though there are a few very helpful ones that can make things so much easier. Generally, a sturdy table is essential. This is important as it will need to support the pounding pressure when hitting punches and stamps with a mallet or maul.

A smooth cutting surface is key, such as a cutting mat. And a strong pounding surface is helpful in absorbing shock and producing a clean cut. For this, a granite slab can work great. with just a few items, the leather working shop will be set to go.

Anvil

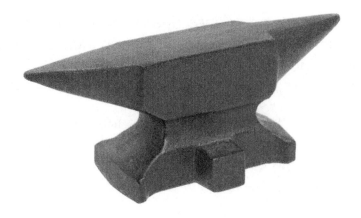

An anvil is a steel or iron tool used mainly as a hitting surface for setting rivets. Most anvils are solid metal, while others can have hollowed-out areas that serve specific purposes. These can include grooves in for straightening metal pieces, or areas for loose hardware or accessory storage. Anvils commonly sit on top of tables or work benches.

Common anvils are solid and usually have a wide, flat surface. They also have a rounded, curved end that tapers into a point. The flat surface is great for hitting on, as it absorbs a lot of the force. The curves end is great for hitting pieces on a unique angle or for shaping curved items.

Anvils are available in many sizes, often denoted by weight. They range in size from a few ounces up to 50+ lbs for larger ones.

Self-Healing Cutting Mats

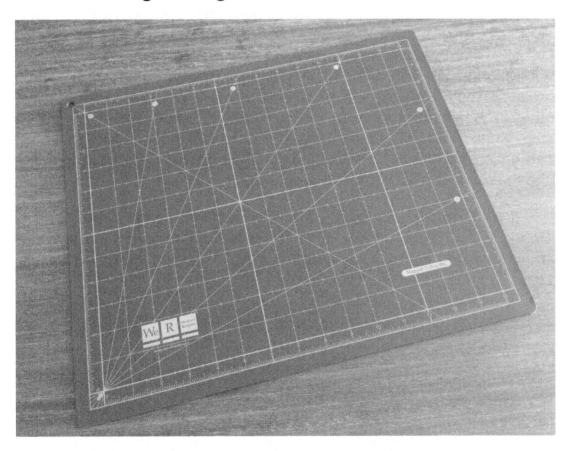

Self-healing cutting mats are specialty-plastic mats comprised a several layers of material that serve as a cutting surface underneath sharp blades. To help ensure the longevity and sharpness of knife blades, it's important to use softer surfaces underneath them when cutting. Harder surfaces could mar or disaffirm the blade.

Cutting mats work great as they are made of layers of materials that will all the knife to sink into them, though not cut all the way through. This protects the knife, and the work surface underneath (such as a desk or table).

Some cutting mats are self-healing, meaning when a knife mark is made during a cut, the plastics in the material will push together mostly eliminating the previous visible cut. In actual practice, different quality mats perform differently in the "self-healing" area, where some real do look like they haven't been cut on, while others look like they've been cut on a million times These mats often come in green and white, with other colors also available. Magnetic cutting mats are an option too. When cutting lighter or thinner materials, magnets can be rested on top of them, securing them from slipping when cutting.

If preferred, cutting mats are also available with measurement markings printed on them. This can make it easier when laying out materials and lining up angles for cuts. A cutting mat is usually a stable leather working tool to have.

Japanese Cutting Mat

Japanese cutting mats are a specialty leather working surface used for cutting and stamping on. They are approximately 1/4" thick, and can provide an "all-in-one" surface for leather crafting.

Where standard cutting mats are thin and great for cutting, sturdier surfaces are usually need to take the pounding of punching, pricking, and chiseling. For this nylon boards or granite slabs can be used. However, this style cutting mat can be used for all of those needs, making it a really useful and versatile leather working surface.

Japanese cutting mats are generally clear in color, and come in various sizes to fit different work areas and preferences. While generally more expensive than self-healing cutting mats, Japanese cutting mats offer more functionality for the leather worker.

Poly Cutting Boards

Poly cutting boards are plastic boards used under leather punching and cutting tools to protect the blades. They absorb impacts and vibrations, and the softness of their material will protect both the cutting blades and the work surface underneath.

When punching leather, it requires a tool to be placed on top of the leather and then hit with a maul or mallet. This drives the blade through the leather and makes the cut. When the blade passes through the leather, it makes contact with the surface underneath. If this surface is metal or very hard, it can damage the cutting blade and make it dull or ineffective.

Placing a poly board under the leather when punching or cutting allows the blade to enter into the softer plastic. This won't harm the blades, and the blade generally does not go through the plastic. This protects the work surface underneath.

These are a very common leather working tool to have, and are available in a wide variety of shapes, thicknesses and colors.

Novolene Chopping Block

A novolene chopping block is a synthetic material formed into a block shape that is used under leather punching and cutting tools to protect the blades. The soft, yet firm material provides a sturdy surface that also helps absorb shock when leather working tools are struck with mallets, hammers, and mauls.

Novolene blocks are generally available in several, rectangular sizes. The color is usually red. This is another option for the leather worker when considering what to use for blade protection and shock absorption for cutting, punching, and stamping activities.

Stone Slabs

Stone slabs are blocks of stone used for shock absorption underneath leather punching, stamping, and cutting tools. The density of the material helps absorb and distribute the hitting forces, while also providing a solid surface on which to perform these tasks.

When stamping, punching, or cutting, a fair amount of downward force is applied through the tools via a hammer, mallet, or maul. This concentrated force is great as it allows the tool's blade to cut smoothly through the leather. However, if the surface it is being performed on is shaky, it could cause less than desirable results or even damage the surface.

Stone is a very dense material, and absorbs shock well. When a stone slab is placed underneath a cutting mat, it is a great punching combination. The cutting mat protects the cutting blades, and the stone slab absorb the hitting force, evenly distributing it through the slab.

Stone slabs are available in a number of sizes and thicknesses, though they don't need to be very large. 6" x 6" is fine, and 12" x 12" provides a bit more force distribution due to its larger size. they really only need to be a bit bigger than the punch or dir being used on top of them.

Quartz is a popular material for stone slabs. Granite also works very well too, as it is a bit denser than quartz, making it's shock absorption performance a little better too. Stone slabs can be purchased, or one might be able to get discarded stone samples from kitchen remodeling or home improvement stores.

Poundo Boards

Poundo boards are rubber surfaces that are used for bade protection or shock absorption in leather working. When cutting or punching with leather tools, the tool blades pass through the leather and onto a surface underneath. If this surface is hard, it could damage the blade. If this surface is soft, the blade goes lightly into the material, protecting the blade and the surface underneath.

These rubber boards come in a variety of sizes, and are usually black in color. They can also be placed underneath a granite or stone slab when punching or pounding, to help with shock absorption.

Leather Tool Holder/Stand

A leather tool holder or stand is a device used to hold and organize leather tools for easy access. They can incorporate a number of holes for placing tools into. They tools stand upright and are easily picked up and put back

There can be multiple levels to the holder, tiered for access to differently-sized tools. They can also have various hole sizes incorporated so tools of different thicknesses or diameters have a secure place to be stored. For example, a maul would be much larger in diameter than a small punch.

Some leather tool holders have uniform holes, such as those that store metal stamp sets. Holders are available in different sizes from small, 12-hole versions, to larger 48+ hole versions.

Leather tools can also be stored in tool boxes or tool drawers. In general, a stand can be most helpful as all tools are always visible and within easy reach.

Cork Board Tool Holder

A cork board tool holder is a material used for holding leather working awls and sewing needles. Cork is a natural, firm material that is easily penetrated by sharp objects. Once inserted, the firmness of the cork generally supports and holds those objects in place.

Leather awls and needles can have very sharp points, and in the case of needles they can be very thin and hard to pick up. Sticking these types of tools upright, into a cork board holder, helps store them tools with their sharp tips embedded into the cork. This is a little safer. It also makes it convenient, as the tools can be easily picked up, used, and returned to their location.

Cork board tool holders are available is a variety of sizes. Usually a helpful shape for leather working is a round, 4" – 6" cork board embedded into a wooden base that sits flat on a desk or work surface. If one finds they have a several awls and many needles all around their workspace, a cork board holder could be a helpful leather working tool to have.

Leather Weights

Leather weights are small metal devices used to hold leather in place when cutting, stamping, or punching. Have smooth, polished surfaces so they will not mark or mar the leather when placed on top of it. They are often made of brass or steel.

When cutting thin leather materials, they can easily shift. Placing metal weights on top can help hold them in place for a stable, more even cut. When cutting thicker leather materials, they might have a natural bend to them. Placing leather weights can help flatten the material into a more even working surface. Leather weights come in various sizes from a few ounces to a few pounds.

Many things can be used as leather weights, as long as their surface does not scratch the leather. If you're looking for well-balanced, nicely-machined, and high-polished weights, dedicated leather weights could be a helpful addition to the leather craft tool list.

Leather Work Apron

A leather work apron is a layer of material worn to protect the clothing underneath it. They generally cover just the front of the person wearing them, and are usually made from leather. A loop goes over the head and secures it behind the neck. A second securing tie goes around the waist.

Work aprons help keep dirt and debris from the work being done from getting onto the person doing the work. They can also protect the wearer from tools that might accidentally get dropped while working. For example, an awl rolls off the table and falls onto their lap. Where a sharply pointed awl might scratch, the apron would provide a layer of protection.

Leather work aprons are available in various sizes, materials, qualities, and finishes. While denim and canvas are options, leather is usually most popular both for the look and for the function of the material.

Some leather aprons also feature various pockets, offering places to hold frequently-accessed tools, pencils, or rulers. While not an essential tool to have when starting out, a leather work apron can be a helpful addition as you become more familiar with leather working and develop preferences for working style and tool storage. And, they look really, really cool.

29 - Conclusion

Leather working tools offer so much in the range of types, styles, and preferences. Over time, you're work to develop your own preferred working style, which will include your favorite tools.

Quality is usually helpful in a tool, when aiming for consistent, great-looking results. With proper care and maintenance, the tools that fill a workshop can perform well, day in and day out for years.

Printed in Great Britain
by Amazon

40528781R00150